THOUGHTS THAT KEEP ME SOBER

Kirk David Carlson

Thoughts That Keep Me Sober
Copyright © 2025 Kirk David Carlson
ISBN: 978-1-964359-20-5
LCCN: 2025902341

All rights reserved. No part of this book may be reproduced, stored in a retrieval system, or transmitted in any form or by any means—electronic, mechanical, digital, photocopy, or any other—without prior permission from the publisher and author, except as provided by the United States of America copyright law.

Unless otherwise noted, all scriptures are from the NEW KING JAMES VERSION®. Copyright© 1982 by Thomas Nelson, Inc. Used by permission. All rights reserved.

Scripture quotations marked (NLT) are taken from the Holy Bible, New Living Translation, copyright ©1996, 2004, 2015 by Tyndale House Foundation. Used by permission of Tyndale House Publishers, Carol Stream, Illinois 60188. All rights reserved.

Address all personal correspondence to:
Kirk Carlson
Email: thoughtsthatkeepmesober@gmail.com

Individuals and church groups may order books from the authors directly, or from the publisher. Retailers and wholesalers should order from our distributors. Refer to the Deeper Revelation Books website for distribution information, as well as an online catalog of all our books.

Published by:
Deeper Revelation Books
Revealing "the deep things of God" (1 Cor. 2:10)
P.O. Box 4260
Cleveland, TN 37320 423-478-2843
Website: www.deeperrevelationbooks.org
Email: info@deeperrevelationbooks.org

Deeper Revelation Books and its divisions assist Christian writers in publishing and distributing their works. Our authors are the ultimate decision-makers in the process. Final responsibility for the creative design, content, permissions, editorial accuracy, stories and doctrinal views, either expressed or implied, belongs to the author. What you hold in your hand is an expression of this author's passion to publish the truth to this generation with a spirit of excellence. It was a blessing and an honor to assist in this process.

ENDORSEMENTS

"I have known Kirk Carlson for years, and I am impressed with how he reaches out to help those with addictions. Kirk has taken responsibility for his actions, and despite his issues of the past, he has become a productive member of society again and supports Law Enforcement. You can feel God's heart in these pages."

Dave Sorenson

"This is a book that undoubtedly will change many lives for the better: wisdom breathes from every page. I have often taught that when God brings someone out of a certain type of darkness, that person earns the right to turn around and deliver others from the same pit. *Thoughts That Keep Me Sober* is strong evidence concerning the validity of that statement. Kirk Carlson doesn't claim to be a theologian, but he is a vessel full of the wisdom of the Father. God does not always call the qualified, but He always qualified the called—and usually He does that through a person's life-experience. Well, if I wore a hat, I would tip it to you Kirk Carlson and shout, "You are truly one of those God-called individuals. Your past could have been a prison; instead, it's become a platform—and God is making your voice to be heard!" It's been a privilege working with you to get this book out to those who need it."

Mike Shreve
CEO (Co-Founder and Chief Enthusiasm Officer)
Deeper Revelation Books

"Kirk has written this book for anyone looking for wisdom and heavenly treasures regarding walking in freedom from alcohol or any addiction. His deep relationship with God and his years in recovery have flowed through his fingers while writing this book."

Rev. G. Sharpe

"*Thoughts That Keep Me Sober* is an exact reflection of author Kirk Carlson. Kirk's giant personality fills every room he is in. He is honest, raw, real, humble, and giving beyond measure. Everyone will enjoy the gift of wisdom he shares in this book."

Kami Barker
Executive Director
Gold Creek Community Church

"I've known Kirk since he first got sober, and the transformation of his life has been a joy to watch. Almost every waking breath is in service to others. *Thoughts That Keep Me Sober* is just one more example of that. Thank you for our journey."

David 'Two Feathers" Fife
Best Friend

"Rarely have I seen a more complete recovery in all my forty-four years of sobriety. From the bottom of the bottle, jails, and car wrecks comes a spiritual deliverance that Dr. Jung would have marveled at. Humble to a fault, he practices our Principles in all his affairs. Hold on to your seat."

Michael R

It is through Kirk's obedience, this book was breathed into life. Kirk has a gift of knowing when God is speaking through people, and by remaining teachable, he allows God to speak through him in his everyday life. Through Kirk's thoughts, actions, and wisdom, he remains a blessing in my life and to those around him. Kirk has blessed my life and my family with his huge heart, willingness to speak truth, and his abundant grace and sense of humor.

Kailah Kilwien
Recovery Coach &
Certified Peer Counselor

DEDICATION

This book is dedicated to all the souls who have struggled, are struggling, or may struggle with the malady of alcoholism and/or drug addiction.

ACKNOWLEDGEMENTS

Special thanks to the members and attendees of the 12x12 Fellowship Hall and Higher Powered at Gold Creek which are the meeting halls where I heard most of these sayings.

This book is written with great gratitude to Jesus Christ, who paid the price for my actions, and to my wife, Waneta Carlson, who stood by me when I was at my worst and held me up when I could not stand. I love you both!

FOREWORD

When Kirk Carlson first shared his idea for this book, *Thoughts That Keep Me Sober*, I knew I could identify. As a fellow traveler on the path of sobriety, I've often found myself struck by the timeless wisdom imparted in the rooms of Alcoholics Anonymous. These clever truths—often delivered with a loving grin by a seasoned old-timer—have a way of embedding themselves in our consciousness. They're the kind of sayings that rise to the top in the middle of the day, whether you're driving down the road or stopped in your tracks in a grocery store aisle. They leave you struck by their profound simplicity that help you course correct throughout your day. God-given treasures that never leave us.

Kirk has an exceptional gift for capturing these moments. His reflections on these pearls of wisdom do more than just recount his journey; they invite you, the reader, to see these truths through a fresh lens. How they apply to yourself and your own life situations. His writing style is both relatable and enlightening, demonstrating how these sayings have not only guided his own sobriety but can also surface truths for others to help in their own recovery. Humbling sayings that provide us a sense of humility that always remind us we're just a bunch of wing nuts on a never-ending path of spiritual growth. The thoughts that kept Kirk sober are not just his own—they came from the godly wisdom of a fellowship that understands the power of openly and honestly sharing their difficult and heart-breaking trials and experiences.

Through his service in Alcoholics Anonymous, his leadership in Advocates Recovery, and his pastoral role at Gold Creek Community Church, Kirk can be defined as trudging, or continually walking with purpose. His tall frame and big boots have led him step-by-step with a compassionate heart always available for service. Along with being a full-time business owner, the sacrifices he and his family endure he humbly sees as, "That's what I'm supposed to do."

In *Thoughts That Keep Me Sober*, Kirk reminds us of those stinging truths we've heard from our sponsors and during shares in meetings—truths that initially right-sized us and continue to humble us as we live one day at a time. Truths that you know are God inspired, because they're never forgotten, and you remember the exact time and place they were delivered. This book isn't just a collection of sayings; it's a toolkit for anyone looking to enrich their journey of recovery. Kirk's unique perspective breathes new life into these old sayings, making them accessible and applicable to anyone who picks up this book.

As someone who has had the privilege of knowing Kirk and witnessing his dedication to recovery, I can attest to the authenticity and heart that underpin every page. His reflections will not only resonate with you but will also challenge you to think differently and apply these insights to your own life. So, as you turn these pages, let Kirk's journey, and the God inspired wisdom guide you on your own path to sobriety.

Doug L.
Member of AA
Reverend
Assistant Director of Northshore Healing Rooms

TABLE OF CONTENTS

Principle 1
ACCEPTANCE 11

Principle 2
FAITH 37

Principle 3
SURRENDER/TRUST 53

Principle 4
HONESTY 77

Principle 5
COURAGE 101

Principle 6
WILLINGNESS 123

Principle 7
HUMILITY 147

Principle 8
FORGIVENESS 171

Principle 9
FREEDOM 193

Principle 10
PERSEVERANCE 225

Principle 11
PATIENCE 253

Principle 12
CHARITY/LOVE 277

ENDNOTES 303

PRINCIPLE 1

ACCEPTANCE

And Jesus said to them, "I am the bread of life. He who comes to Me shall never hunger, and he who believes in Me shall never thirst."
(John 6:35)

MY ALCOHOLISM IS STALKING ME.

I live on seven acres. Part of my property is fenced so the dogs don't disappear into the woods. The lower portion is kept open, so the wildlife can migrate back and forth between the pond, creek, and landscaping. I don't want to stop them from getting on and off my property or block their path from mountain to sea. It's actually beautiful, with all types of land, air, and water life.

Sometimes, I walk my fence line with Sergeant, my 110-pound, English Cream Golden Retriever. Coyotes are abundant on our property, and sometimes, as we walk, a coyote will trail us. Coyotes weigh about thirty-five pounds, so neither my dog nor I are bothered, but we are alert. If I, or my dog, get tired of the stalking by the coyote, the slightest movement I allow Sergeant to make towards it sends it fleeing at full pace. The coyote is no match for my dog.

That's a great picture for me of my alcoholism. My dog is like my sobriety, and the coyote is like my alcoholism. I know it's there, but it doesn't bother me as long as I'm walking with my solution. Sergeant is my solution to the coyote, and sobriety is my solution to alcoholism. My alcoholism is no match for my sobriety, so long as I walk with my solution always close by.

NINETY MEETINGS IN NINETY DAYS.

Sounds pretty straightforward. Not a lot of thinking to that one. Go to ninety meetings in ninety days. Why? Isn't that overkill? Do I really need a meeting every day for three months? Surely, if I just don't drink, I'll be alright. If I get squirrely, and thoughts about drinking come into my mind, I can always go to a meeting. I don't need ninety meetings in ninety days, do I?

All I know is this—when I was sober for just a few days, I heard it said, that I should do ninety in ninety, o just try it. So, I did. It made everything else easier. I didn't drink one day at a time just because I had a meeting to go to. Not drinking stopped the madness.

Without new madness to contend with, old madness started falling off. Ninety meetings in ninety days caused me to almost automatically live the program. It was steadily a part of my life and was on the way to being my new way of life. By the time ninety days were up, I was thinking clearly. Life, so to speak, was settling down. Things that were foggy were becoming clear again, and I was starting to make rational decisions once more. It was working so well; I decided to do another ninety in ninety.

One day, I was talking to my grand sponsor, and he had a science magazine with some kind of picture of two brains on the front of it. The brain on the left was blue with yellow all over it, blocking rational reason areas and such. The one on the right was blue with only a few yellow spots. It was the same brain after being alcohol free for ninety days. Go figure! Science and reality agree—ninety meetings in ninety days!

MY LIFE WAS DETERIORATING FASTER THAN I COULD LOWER MY STANDARDS.

For quite a while, I was able to adjust my drinking to keep my major problems at bay. However, I didn't really adjust my drinking; I adjusted my issues to give myself the appearance that I was still okay. There was always someone worse than me. I would tell myself, "If I ever do that, if I ever get as bad as that guy, or if that ever happened to me, etc. then I'll stop drinking."

The problem was, when I did "that," or when I ended up "as bad as that guy," or when that "happened to me," I would just lower my standards. No problem here, I'm still not as bad as that other guy, and this, that, or the other thing that's happened to me. Every time my life deteriorated, I'd simply lower my standards. I wasn't at the bottom ... yet.

As my life of drugs and alcohol increased, so did my issues. My issues at home, at work, with friends, even my legal and financial issues kept getting worse and worse. Lowering my standards became almost a daily event. The spiral down was becoming a straight drop. I found my life deteriorating faster than I could lower my standards. I couldn't catch up with the fall, and I hit bottom with a thud.

That was the eye-opener for me and possibly my life-saving grace. There were no standards of life left to lower. Forced to my knees, due to the inability to stand on my own two feet any longer, I felt the hand of God touch me and tell me I was going to be okay. I was guided to Alcoholics Anonymous, with little understanding of what had touched me and how I had been guided there. Now, all I really know is, since getting there, my life has changed. I am constantly moving upward and seem to have a purpose. I have standards today, and my life no longer deteriorates.

ON A GOOD DAY, WE'RE ALL FIVE YEARS OLD. ON A BAD DAY, WE'RE ALL FIVE YEARS OLD AND TERRIFIED.

I have pretty much settled into the fact that I know but only a portion, so I'm encouraged that more will be revealed. There is a book titled, *All I Really Need to Know I Learned in Kindergarten*. That's when we are five years old. So, on a good day, that's all I need to know, for now. As more is revealed, my knowledge expands. On a bad day, I feel the limits of myself, and I am terrified.

I don't think that book really expects that nothing else needs to be learned after paying close attention in kindergarten. Basically, it refers to the foundation of our character. In kindergarten, we are taught to tell the truth. We are taught lessons like do not lie, be polite, say please, say thank you, be respectful, obey authority, obey police, obey teachers, obey adults, take care of your hygiene, wash up, brush your teeth, etc. All the basic rules that produce a life of good character and productivity were taught to me in kindergarten when I was five years old.

On a good day, I walk in those truths, and they propel me into the successes of that day. However, at five years old, I lacked maturity and experience, and navigating some aspects of life was terrifying. However, the knowledge I learned from the foundation that was built through simple, basic rules from kindergarten empowers me now to step out of the fear and find the solution. Remembering the basics of the foundation of my life allows me to progress forward without losing sight of the truths.

ONCE YOU'RE A PICKLE, YOU CAN NEVER BECOME A CUCUMBER AGAIN.

That makes sense! That's actually something I can understand. If you take a cucumber and pickle it, it's a pickle. It's no longer a cucumber, and it can never be one again. That's me. I'm a pickle, and I can never be a cucumber again!

When I first started drinking, I didn't know I was an alcoholic. I just knew it made me feel awesome, and all my inhibitions disappeared. I was on top of the world, my world, and it felt perfect. As life went on, my drinking went on too. Pretty soon, it was part of my everyday life. Even when it wasn't planned, I always seemed to end up drunk.

I lost all control of my choices once I touched alcohol, and I couldn't seem to not touch it. I was drinking against my own will. I would try to drink normal, but it wasn't possible. The very touch of alcohol to my lips sent me to the uncontrollable phenomenon of craving. I had drunk to the point of pickling myself. I finally realized that I could never be a cucumber again, so I better learn to live as a pickle.

PRINCIPLE 1—ACCEPTANCE

PEOPLE WANT TO BE
ACCEPTED, LOVED, AND HEARD.

This is something I can totally understand, so why am I so terrible at it? Part of the reason I drank was to feel accepted and definitely, to be heard. I was much more outspoken when loaded. My voice carried even more. As far as being loved, I never gave too many people a reason to love me. Sure, I was the life of the party on several occasions, bringing joy and laughter to many, but truly loved, I was never worthy of that.

As long as I stayed drunk though, I didn't really care. At least not till I sobered up and felt sorry for myself. So, knowing personally that I want to be accepted, loved, and heard should cause me to extend that same courtesy to others. After all, when those things are extended to me, it affects my life for the better.

Somehow, after years of sobriety, the struggle with this has become easier. As I've been accepted for who I am, as opposed to what I've done, I find that having some patience and understanding with others is possible. It's been a process that I first had to accept for myself, but as others have accepted, loved, and heard the broken me, I've found the ability to accept, love, and hear others.

Our program is one of progress, not perfection. As long as I keep coming around, I find constant progression in my relationship to others. When I accept, love, and hear others, it is my life that progresses.

SOME OF US HAVE TO DIE,
SO THAT THE REST OF US CAN LIVE.

It's a sad truth, but nonetheless, it is the truth! Unfortunately, most of us in AA have a built-in forgetter. We go along sober for a while, and then, one day, often for no apparent reason, we go back out, usually never making it back into a program of recovery. I'm sure I have one more drunk left in me, but I'll never use it.

Although I have another drunk in me, I don't have another recovery in me. Thus, I will never use again! I can't. As sad as it is, I have learned this from watching others go back out and either die instantly or die trying to get back to the program and a path of recovery. Some of us have to die, so that the rest of us can live.

PRINCIPLE 1—ACCEPTANCE

WHAT HAPPENS IF WE
DON'T WORK THE AA PROGRAM?

I know what Alcoholics Anonymous says are the promises we receive if we work the program and are painstaking about it. But what happens if we don't work the program of Alcoholics Anonymous or are not painstaking about it? When I saw this list, I thought it was worth pointing out.

It seems to be the reverse promises: "If we are not painstaking about this phase of our development, we will be drunk before we leave the parking lot. We are going to know a new pain and a new misery. We will regret our deeds and repeat them over and over. We will comprehend the word chaos, and we will know calamity. No matter how far down the road we stagger, we will still wonder where we are going. That feeling of uselessness and self-pity will intensify. We will lose interesting things and gain relations with strange fellows. Self-seeking will be constant. Our whole attitude will be on the lookout for the cops, fear of people, and economic security will leave us homeless. We will intuitively know how to stay drunk with little or no money. We will suddenly begin to think that God does not exist. Are these extravagant promises? Probably not. They are being practiced daily, sometimes insanely, sometimes deadly. They will continue to happen if we keep drinking."

Work the program thoroughly, and with help, and you will receive the Ninth Step Promises, not the reverse promises.

TURNS OUT MY ROCK BOTTOM HAD A TRAP DOOR.

Every time I hit rock bottom in my drinking career, I would simply lower the bar. There was always someone worse than me. If they hadn't hit bottom yet, then I could just lower mine. When I got to where they were, I'd notice someone else even more down on their life and lower my bottom again. I got to be pretty darn good with a shovel and quite capable of digging my hole deeper and deeper.

As my life deteriorated more and more, as I lost possessions, relationships, jobs, my standing in society, respect from others, and even my self-respect, the hole just got deeper. At some point, it became too much, and I hit rock bottom. I simply couldn't handle life as it was anymore. Then it happened, I met someone who was as pathetic as I could ever imagine, and I dropped lower again. It turns out my rock bottom had a trap door.

I fell right through it. I learned to find sanctuary in my own squalor. If this was the destiny of my life, I'd better learn how to accept it. Fortunately, by the grace of God, something inside me wouldn't allow me to accept it. Deep within me was a pain I couldn't live with, and it was time to just end it all or change it all.

With little hope, I got a sponsor in Alcoholics Anonymous and purposed to follow the path that he showed me. I ended up slowly climbing out of the hole I had dug. Pretty soon, I was on top of that trap door and could see the daylight above. For once, the light at the end of the tunnel wasn't the oncoming train. With the help of the fellowship in our program, and a loving Higher Power whom I call God, I'm out of the hole. If you're going down in life, put away the shovel, stop digging, and watch out for the trap door.

THE ONLY THING I CAN REALLY CONTROL IS MY ATTITUDE.

Shouldn't I be better at it if it's the only thing I have power over? If my attitude is the only thing I can really control, you'd think I would have mastered it by now, but that's not the case. Working on it is a daily chore. For some reason, my attitude can snap in an instant.

I'm better at controlling it than I used to be, but I have to be careful not to use that as justification when it's bad. Saying, "At least I'm not as bad as I was," is sometimes my rationalization to accept a bad attitude. If I'm not careful, a poor attitude can become a comfort zone.

When I'm not behaving right, it's easy to justify and rationalize my actions while holding on to an attitude that's contrary to my own best interests. While my bad attitude can certainly bring others down, I'm the one that's affected most. It's my joy and serenity that disappears. I'm a sick person with a disease that strives to keep me ill. Daily effort is necessary to combat the power that works against me.

The good news is that I have access to a Power greater than that. If I seek God daily, my disease doesn't stand a chance. His power and guidance displace my bad attitude as soon as it shows itself, if I let it. The key is to go to Him first, each and every morning, and ask for His attitude to overwhelm mine. On my own, I'm powerless, but with God's help, I can control my attitude.

THE MORE I LEARN, THE MORE I REALIZE HOW LITTLE I KNOW.

When I first came into Alcoholics Anonymous, I knew nothing about the program. I simply knew that I didn't want to drink anymore, and I hoped the program could help me. After thirty days of sobriety, I had figured it out. See, I'm a smart guy, so it wasn't going to take me years to get it. When I hit sixty days, I realized that I really didn't understand a lot at thirty days, but now I see more clearly.

At ninety days, I realized that at sixty days in, I hadn't known squat, but now I had an understanding. When I reached six months of my sobriety, I found I was quite inadequate at ninety days, and my life was now going to be better as I knew and understood how the program worked. When I reached one year, I realized how little I knew at six months.

Now, several years later, I actually realize how little I know. Like our book teaches us, "I KNOW ONLY A LITTLE, MORE WILL BE REVEALED." I need to continue to come to meetings, or I will never know that which is yet to be revealed.

THE GOOD NEWS IS, THIS IS IT.
THE BAD NEWS IS, THIS IS IT.

Finally, a solution. What good news that was to see. This is it. After years of struggle, trying everything I could think of to overcome my obsession with alcohol, I was at a place where there was a solution. I'd been to seven inpatient treatments, several jail terms, sworn off drugs and alcohol on workdays, at home, away from home, or you name it. But finally, upon landing in Alcoholics Anonymous, I was shown a solution. It was simple. Not necessarily easy, but simple. Then it hit me—this is it?

Really! No other successful solution exists for me. I'm destined to live life as a degenerate drunk or live life in the hall of Alcoholics Anonymous till I die. Isn't that bad news as far as my future goes? Maybe for some, but I've found that the good news of being a member of Alcoholics Anonymous, living life sober, far outweighs the bad news of never being able to drink again. As it turns out, it's just all good news for this alcoholic.

THE FATAL MALADY—"ALCOHOLISM"— MADNESS AND DEATH ARE ITS FRUITS

I can put my alcoholism in remission, I can recover, but I can't be cured. At least not at the time of this writing. If I stop for a period, and start back up again, I'm still the same alcoholic I was before ever quitting. It's absolutely mind-boggling. My alcoholism seems to have one goal—to drive me mad and bury me.

As with many other medical conditions that have no cure, it doesn't mean life has to end. One of my sons and one of my daughters have diabetes. They need insulin, in some form daily, to stay alive and well. I have alcoholism, I need recovery, in some form daily, to stay alive and well. My disease is progressive and fatal. I will die an alcoholic, but I don't have to die drunk, mad, and insane.

I have learned, through painstaking experiences, that alcoholism is a fatal malady whose fruits are madness and death. I have also learned that I don't have to eat from that tree. I look at alcohol as the tree of forbidden fruit. They found madness and death too. Stay away from forbidden fruit.

THE ABCS OF RECOVERY— ATTITUDE, BEHAVIOR, CHOICES

Those are the same ABCs that got me in trouble. My attitude, my behavior, and my choices, so I definitely know how to do my ABCs. Now, I just needed to use them for my recovery, instead of my demise. In everything that I do in life, my attitude tends to determine the outcome. When I feel discouraged, success is difficult. If I keep a positive attitude, things are easier to overcome.

Life has good and bad aspects. My attitude towards it directly impacts my success or failure navigating it. Growing up, I used to hear, "Mind your Ps and Qs." Its origin is questionable, but its meaning is not. Basically, it means mind your manners or be on your best behavior.

When I was drinking and drugging, I had no manners, and my behavior was however I felt like acting. It was always about what I wanted and nothing else. As my attitude changed, so did my behavior. Maybe I wasn't such a bad guy after all. Before sobriety, I made all my choices based on what I wanted, what made me happy, and what got me something. When I renewed my attitude about life, drugs, alcohol, and God, I could just see how backwards and destructive my behavior was.

Once I could see this clearly, it was simple to make choices that uplifted my life and spirit. I now embrace the ABCs of recovery with my attitude, behavior, and choices guided by the hand of God, my Higher Power, instead of trying to manage them on my own.

LET US LOVE YOU TILL YOU LEARN TO LOVE YOURSELF.

When I got to Alcoholics Anonymous, I wasn't in much of a condition to love myself. I didn't even like myself. I had left my faith, I had abandoned my family, I had run my business into the ground, and I had found myself broke, alone, and homeless. I had no car, no license, and no self-respect. Loving myself wasn't exactly something I felt like doing. In fact, it wasn't something I was even capable of doing.

The first time I heard, "Let us love you till you learn to love yourself," I thought it was a joke. Yeah! Let's all hold hands and sing "Kumbaya" too. I didn't get it. I was truly incapable of loving myself, and everyone in AA knew it. Of course, they knew. They had all been where I was, and there was a time when they didn't love themselves either.

They knew I wasn't worthless; I just felt that way. I couldn't get sober while I felt this way. Alcohol is what I used to keep from facing myself. I couldn't change the way I felt until I got sober. What in the world was I to do? I figured I better let them love me till I learned to love myself, and they did!

People in AA seemed to know the value in me that I couldn't see. They lifted me up when I couldn't stand on my perceived worth. They gave me the strength to believe that I had value while I just worked on not drinking. The more sober I became, the more I understood, and the more I started to see my own value. In the house of AA, I was loved until I learned to love myself. This program rocks!

JUST CAUSE YOU SLEEP IN THE GARAGE, IT DOESN'T MAKE YOU A CAR.

We have a simple program, but it wasn't always easy. There's work involved in sobriety. You can't catch it like some kind of happenstance. For quite some time, I went to meetings in Alcoholics Anonymous, and nothing happened, nothing changed. I'd walk out of the meeting, usually with my wife, and off to the bar we'd go. We would talk about the sick people we saw at those meetings. They were either in bad shape or certainly had been.

After lots of legal issues that drove me to the brink of insanity with incarceration, it was either quit drinking or live life behind bars, if I survived. For months, I sat in meetings, listening to what was said about alcohol, its progression, my lack of choice while using, and even the hope and often joy that others had found there. Still, nothing clicked.

The pain of life was the same, except for the mild reprieve I had while in the meetings. I faithfully attended meetings, hoping to catch this elusive thing called sobriety, and I'd walk out lost. Then, I heard it. Someone said, "Just cause you sleep in the garage, it doesn't make you a car." Somehow, there was a click in my brain, and I understood it.

Going to meetings and doing nothing was fruitless. Faith without works is dead. I couldn't gain sobriety by osmosis. Still lost, I decided I needed to put out effort if I was to have any hope. I got a sponsor, followed his suggestions, and a miracle happened. All I had to do was my part, and God handled the rest.

I'M NOT RESPONSIBLE FOR MY FIRST THOUGHT, BUT I AM RESPONSIBLE FOR MY SECOND.

Sometimes, thoughts come into my head, and my first response is, "Where the heck did that come from?" It happens, and for some reason, it's the bad, negative thoughts that seem to pop up. Suddenly, out of nowhere, a drink sounds good, or a woman looks nice, or that thing the other guy has becomes my desire. It happens, right out of the blue.

That's not where the problem arises. We can throw the thought out of our heads, or think the drink through, or any of the dozens of other positive responses. The problem comes when the second thought backs up the improper desire. It's the second thought that drives to our action. I don't know where some of these thoughts come from. The thoughts sort of just appear from time to time. It's like the devil is trying to pull me down and keep me from doing the right thing.

The important aspect is what we do about the negative thoughts when they come. Do we counter it with the proper resistance? Or do we give into it and all the temptation? It's not the first thought that characterizes who I am and what I'll become. It's the second thought, and for that, I am responsible.

IF YOU'VE GOT IT, YOU'RE NEVER GOING TO GET RID OF IT (ALCOHOLISM).

That's not exciting news. As with any unwanted disease, the goal is always to get rid of it. A clean bill of health is preferable. So, what do you do if you have a disease that can't be cured? Are you supposed to just live with it? Isn't that kind of hopeless? Figuring out how to live with alcoholism wasn't something I wanted to do. I wanted to eliminate it from my life all together.

The more I learned about the disease, the more I realized I couldn't eliminate alcoholism from my life. However, I could eliminate alcohol from my life. That was the key. As long as I didn't drink any alcohol, the destruction of my life from alcoholism was nonexistent. It was like putting my disease in remission.

Having alcoholism wasn't such a big deal once I realized I had it, embraced it, and sought to recover from it. I no longer have to worry about my disease because I've learned how to live with it. By facing it head on, and helping others do the same, I have solved the drink problem. Today, I live in recovery, one day at a time, and find joy within the midst of my disease.

FIRST THINGS FIRST

Ever feel like you're getting the cart before the horse? Maybe you've got things a little out of order. You won't be able to get your life together until you start making better decisions. You can't make better decisions until you put the plug in the jug and stop drinking. You can't stop drinking until you surrender to the fact that you're an alcoholic.

It goes way beyond just stopping drinking though. In everything I do, I need to put certain things first. This isn't something that is difficult to do, if I put one foot in front of the other and do the next indicated thing. Life doesn't usually come at me sideways, and the next first thing to put first is simply the thing in front of me.

I often want to get to the finish point without going through all the motions it takes. When I attempt this, the results are always incomplete. A lot of putting first things first is so basic, we take it for granted, or don't even realize we do it.

I must start the car before I can drive it; I must turn on the stove before my vegetables will cook, etc. We get so used to it that we tend to not pay attention when it counts. There is purpose for the order of everything in life, so we need to make sure that we put first things first in everything we do, especially when it comes to the matter of our sobriety.

I MIGHT NOT BE MUCH,
BUT I'M ALL I THINK ABOUT.

How do you possibly go through life as a self-indulged alcoholic without thinking about yourself? Even sober I can't help but think of myself. The airlines taught me to put my mask on first. If I don't take care of myself, what will I have to offer anyone else? How can I be of use to another if I'm not in appropriate shape myself?

For the most part, that's OK, so long as I'm taking care of myself for the purpose of helping others. It's not a bad thing to better myself, as long as I'm not selfish in my desire to. The more money I have, the more there is to help another person in need. The greater my health is, the longer I can help others. The stronger my spirit is, the more hope I can bring to others. The better my life is, in every aspect of it, the more service I am able to do for others. If I have a lack of everything in my life, I probably can't help anybody.

The key to this is to maintain an unselfish life. The Third Step Prayer asks God to take away my difficulties but not to make my life easier and more pleasureful. It goes on to say that victory over them would bear witness to those I would help of thy power, thy love, and thy way of life. I take care of myself daily, but I do it to be of service, not to be served.

EACH MORNING WHEN I WAKE UP, I'M THANKFUL FOR THREE THINGS I AM NOT— I AM NOT DEAD, I AM NOT DRUNK, AND I AM NOT IN CHARGE,

I own my own business. Sometimes, I love it, and sometimes, I hate it. A lot of people have a misconception about being in charge, and trust me, it's not all it's cracked up to be. The weight on your shoulders wears you down. Sometimes, your employees and customers expect you to carry the world. I often wondered if that was part of why I drank. Mostly it was because I am an alcoholic.

Anyway, my control issues weren't contained to work. I seemed to have an opinion about everything, and it was tiring. For quite a while, drinking helped. It made relaxing the stress easier and quicker, but once I was fully engulfed by my alcoholism, I was just drunk.

I hated every morning because I woke up to the same wrecked life that I started drinking to get away from. The pain never subsided because my drinking never did. I started doing cocaine, so I could drink longer without passing out. After a while, I started having issues with my heart. I couldn't quit drinking and drugging, even though I was staring death in the face.

Somehow, I found myself in the halls of Alcoholics Anonymous, and by the grace of God and fellowship of the program, I am sober today. I no longer wake up terrified, grab a drink, take a hit, and get on with my day. Now, I wake up thankful for three things: I am not dead, I am not drunk, and I am not in charge.

PRINCIPLE 1—ACCEPTANCE

IT'S THE LOCOMOTIVE THAT KILLS YOU, NOT THE CABOOSE.

Personally, I don't want to get hit by any part of a train, so I stay off the tracks they run on. However, I do realize that the first train car to hit me is the one that's going to take me out. The same can be said of my drinking. All is lost in my life if I take that first drink. I don't have to wait for the last one, the first one will erase all the progress I have made.

Just like with the locomotive, I don't want to try and dodge the outcome, so I simply stay off the tracks. I used to think taking chances was kind of exciting, but after a few lessons of life, I found there were better ways for me to find joy and excitement. Trying to cheat death on the railroad tracks has taken the life out of many seeking excitements, just as trying to cheat death as an alcoholic has too.

Everyday drinking had become life standing on the tracks, waiting for the train to come. Often it was more hoping for the train to come. Now, after being sober a while, I stay off the tracks where the trains of my addiction run. I don't even flirt with that first drink because I know it's the locomotive that will kill me, not the caboose.

ALCOHOLISM IS A PHYSICAL ADDICTION AND A MENTAL OBSESSION.

Alcohol had become something I had to have. It wasn't always that I wanted it, but I had to have it. The mental obsession would literally give me a headache. I couldn't stop thinking about my next drink if I didn't have one. The compulsion to drink was overbearing. It had become impossible for me to resist the desire to drink. I thought my mind would explode without alcohol. On top of that, if I went too long without alcohol, I would shake. It was as if my body wouldn't cooperate if there wasn't some amount of alcohol in it. The thought of going through life without alcohol felt like a lot of pain and headache. Honestly, staying loaded seemed easier. Not so much easier, just less painful.

However, the pain of my active alcoholism had finally overtaken my fear of sobriety. When I finally found my way into Alcoholics Anonymous, I was at the point of surrender. There was no fight left in me. That was probably a good thing. It made listening to other people's suggestions possible. I had no solution myself, so it certainly couldn't hurt to follow the suggestions of those who claimed to find a solution.

The longer I hung around, the more I understood malady. Abstinence was the only solution, and I couldn't do that on my own. Alcoholism is a physical addiction and a mental obsession, and without understanding that, I haven't got a chance. Knowing that empowers me to seek the solution, and embracing the fellowship of Alcoholics Anonymous has allowed me to recover from both. As long as I stay abstinent from alcohol, and present in fellowship, the physical addiction and mental obsession are subdued.

PRINCIPLE 1—ACCEPTANCE

ALCOHOL IS NOT THE PROBLEM. I AM.

I don't seem to have as many issues when I'm sober as I do when I'm drunk. Doesn't that mean alcohol is the problem? Not really. However, my drinking is. Alcohol just sits there in its bottle, not affecting anyone or anything. As soon as I partake in drinking it though, an ugliness appears that overtakes me.

It wasn't always that way, but signs of it were there from the very first drink I ever had. I used alcohol to hide who I was, change who I was, or simply forget who I was. When life was turned upside down, I used alcohol to turn it back over. The problem was, it just caused me to turn over, and over, and over again, not realizing that it was actually my life rolling downhill, faster and faster. I didn't want to look in the mirror and face who I was, and the alcohol made that possible.

I could quit periodically, but I couldn't stay quit. The life I was living was painful and hard, and I couldn't seem to change it, so alcohol became my friend. Bad choice. At some point, my life was in such despair that I couldn't continue. Somehow, I ended up in Alcoholics Anonymous, and was told that I was the problem, not the alcohol.

I didn't understand that. I wasn't even sure if I believed it, but by going to meetings and listening to others, I managed to stop drinking. It was after that I was able to see my part in it all. Alcohol had been masking my problems all along. It became clear that alcohol was not the real problem—I was. I also realized that I couldn't fix the problems while drowning them in alcohol. Sobriety allows me to face and fix the problem—me.

ALCOHOL IS BUT A SYMPTOM.

Alcohol was not my problem. It was my solution. It was my solution to everything, and I was the problem. I couldn't accept life as it was. I wanted to put an exclamation point on every aspect of it. When things went well, alcohol was the choice to celebrate. When things went wrong, alcohol consoled me. If I didn't have the courage to tackle a situation, alcohol gave it to me. Alcohol could solve any problem I had and any problem I came across. When it worked, it worked well, but at some point, it quit working.

It no longer solved anything, even temporarily. I finally realized it never really solved anything, it just masked it or postponed it. As I came to realize that I was the problem, I found I was stuck on alcohol. The very thing I had used to solve my problems was now keeping me from addressing them. I needed to change my life, and the only hope in doing that was to put down the alcohol.

Alcoholics Anonymous helped me see clearly as I heard the solutions in meeting after meeting after meeting. Alcohol was really no solution at all! At least not for me, because I AM AN ALCOHOLIC, and life is unmanageable when I drink.

PRINCIPLE 2

FAITH

And the prayer of faith will save the sick, and the Lord will raise him up. And if he has committed sins, he will be forgiven. (James 5:15)

PULLED BY THE VISION, NOT PUSHED BY THE PAIN.

Life had become totally unmanageable. My outlook on life was basically nonexistent. It didn't matter how I looked at it, the reality was that life just sucked. I wasn't making decisions and moving in this or that direction. I went wherever in life the pain pushed me. Ninety-nine percent of the time that included alcohol or some other mind or body-altering substance.

It got to the point where I was simply being pushed around in life. Decisions weren't made, instead, life just stumbled on. At some point, I found myself stuck in the pain. There wasn't a substance that could relieve the pain any longer. Completely out of solutions, the pain pushed me into treatment. Treatment pushed me into Alcoholics Anonymous. Alcoholics Anonymous pushed me into service work. I was still getting pushed around.

After a while of doing service work, I found I was still staying sober. I saw things of worth in others, and I wanted that for myself. Desires were building up inside of me, and I found myself being pulled by the vision ahead, instead of being pushed by the pain of the past. Service to others had pushed me into fellowship, and that fellowship gave me a vision that has pulled me through life with absolute serenity and comfort with who I am and why I exist. Today, I am pulled by the vision, not pushed by the pain.

PRAYER AND MEDITATION

For me, prayer is talking to God, and meditation is listening to Him. Unfortunately, I seem to be much better at prayer than I am at meditation. Don't get me wrong, prayer is not only good, it's essential, but God gave me one mouth and two ears, so I tend to believe He wants me to listen more than talk.

This has always been a struggle. I know I'm usually not the smartest person in the room, yet I also know I'm usually the most outspoken. Even in my prayer closet, I talk more than I listen. After all, it's a prayer closet, not a meditation closet.

Sometimes, I think I don't hear as well, because I have a predetermined idea or expectation of the answer to my prayer. When the answer or solution comes, it's not what I'm expecting, so I don't even notice it. It passes right by me because I'm not even listening for an answer, instead I'm waiting for a result.

I pray for my finances to change; the answer is to get a job. I hear nothing and wonder why I'm broke. I pray for my sickness to heal; the answer is go to the doctor. I hear nothing and wonder why I'm still sick. I pray to be sober, yet I don't put down the bottle, when that answer is obvious.

My prayer life is sincere, but my meditation isn't. It's not on purpose, but it is fact. I need to be just as sincere in my meditation as I am in my prayers.

WITH GOD ALL THINGS ARE POSSIBLE.

Man was I glad to hear that! All I knew when I got to the end of my rope was that nothing seemed possible. I couldn't complete a single task except getting loaded. Alcohol had me by the privates and wouldn't let go. Not only was I overwhelmed with each individual responsibility, but life itself was getting to be impossible. Fat, drunk, and stupid wasn't working out like it used to. Alcohol had won. Its power could no longer be eluded. It was simply stronger than I was.

When I came into Alcoholics Anonymous though, I was told I could have hope. I was told and showed "How It Works." In "How It Works," I'm told there is One who has all power—that One is God. Add that to, "With God all things are possible," and I found hope. It's true that I couldn't win this battle on my own, but I didn't have to fight it.

I have found that God will fight for me if I simply show up, but I have to show up suited, booted, and ready to roll up my sleeves. My God isn't lazy, sitting around playing video games and ignoring life. He's busy giving life to those who seek His help. I'm acutely aware of my limitations, as they are vast. However, I only need to show up and be ready to do what is set before me. As I do my part, I find God does His, but I always have to do my part. God doesn't do it all for me; He does it with me. Moreover, I do it with God, because then, all things are possible.

YOU CAN'T BE HATEFUL IF YOU'RE GRATEFUL.

This rings true in so many aspects of my life. When I walk around feeling grateful, nothing seems to be too difficult to overcome. I don't get mad at situations. Instead, I stay positive and continue to work through them. Feeling good breeds more feeling good.

Things are going to happen to me, and people are going to do things to me I don't like. As long as I focus on the things that I'm grateful for, hate won't dwell in my mind and resentments won't build up. Life is so much better being grateful for what I do have, rather than being hateful about everything that doesn't please me. For starters, I'm not in jail; I'm not in an institution, and I'm not dead. That's a whole heck of a lot to be grateful for.

Having an attitude of gratitude has changed my life. When I get hateful, I build up resentments. Resentments always hurt me, not the person, place, or situation I'm resentful towards. Try it for yourself and see if it proves to be true or not. You can't be hateful if you're grateful.

PRAYER: A BRIDGE BETWEEN PANIC AND PEACE

Drinking held back the panic, but it definitely did not produce any peace. The longer I suppressed the panic, the further away the peace was. By the time I was done drinking, I not only didn't know where the peace was, but I didn't even know what peace was. It had eluded me for so long, that I wasn't sure it could ever exist in my life again. Chaos was my plight in life.

As I stayed sober, day after day, the chaos seemed to subside. The panic didn't disappear altogether, but when I prayed, I could feel peace. I wasn't sure where it was, but I knew I could feel it. It was definitely within reach. I have found that when I walk closer to God, there is more peace in my life and far less panic.

If I don't seek God's will for my life, I'm simply running my own will. That's what got me into trouble in the first place. On the other hand, if I seek God's will for my life through prayer and meditation, my spirit is put at ease. When I pray, I bridge the gap, and I am able to cross over from panic to peace.

WHAT WE REALLY HAVE IS A DAILY REPRIEVE CONTINGENT ON THE MAINTENANCE OF OUR SPIRITUAL CONDITION.

What does that mean? I quit drinking because alcohol was ruining my life. What has my spiritual condition got to do with that? It was the booze that was the problem. Eliminate that and the problem would be solved. The issue was—I couldn't stop drinking.

With every passing day, it got more and more painful. Eventually, my spirit was broken, and life wasn't much worth living. Legal issues mounted, and I was pretty much forced into attending AA meetings. If I didn't go, they were going to put me back in jail, so I went. As I continued to go, something started happening inside me. I found that when I was in a meeting, surrounded by the fellowship, my very inner self felt content. My spirit had energy and goodwill. I could feel life. I didn't want to drink.

In fact, while I was there, I didn't think about drinking. It turns out that when my spiritual well-being is in good order, altering it just isn't desirable. If I don't want to drink, I don't have to, but that isn't quite as easy as it sounds. Even at fifteen years sober, I go through trials that can be overwhelming and thoughts, not good ones, come rushing in. However, they no longer take me down, because my program includes the maintenance of my spiritual condition, and with that, I am given a daily reprieve.

SPIRITUAL EXPERIENCE

Everybody's spiritual experience is different. It's personal to each one of us, touching on just what God has in store for our individual lives, depending on where we come from and where we're heading. For me, it was a very distinct, visual picture. I've had many since that first one, and for me, they all seem to have a visual picture to the vision I get. They have all been powerful, but I cherish and live by my first.

It was a simple vision. I saw the world as my Father's house. That makes for a pretty big home with lots of room in it. I also saw the people of the world as guests in my Father's house. However, I didn't see myself as the number one son in that house. I didn't see myself as one of His children. I saw myself as a servant of His house. My vision was to take care of the guests in my Father's house.

I have settled into that role with a gladness that I sometimes don't understand. Don't get me wrong, I'm not a saint, and I don't always jump for joy at this vision. But I do believe it has given me a purpose-driven life. If someone comes to me for help, whether that's spiritual, physical, mental, emotional, financial, or anything else, my job is to fulfill that need. If I'm not able to, I go to my Father and seek His guidance on where to point them. Accepting my spiritual experience as God's will for me has enabled me to live a life of fulfillment. I'm glad He gives me direction daily.

PRINCIPLE 2—FAITH

WE DON'T HAVE TO DRINK,
EVEN IF WE WANT TO.

One of my problems has been that I tend to give into my desires, even if I know they are not good for me. I still want what I want and give into the yearning. Drinking was just something I did. Nobody forced me; I drank because I wanted to.

In Alcoholics Anonymous, I found I didn't have to drink, even if I wanted to. If I want a drink, or even think of having one, I can call a friend in the program, go to a meeting, or just read some literature to ease my mind. I have been given tools to deal with those things that make me uncomfortable and the feeling of want that I have. I DON'T HAVE TO DRINK, EVEN IF I WANT TO!

TWO THINGS ABOUT PRAYER—YOU HAVE TO START AND YOU HAVE TO CONTINUE.

My life has completely changed since incorporating prayer into it on a daily basis. I've always believed in the power of prayer. I've always believed God heard my prayers, even believed that they got answered, although I usually missed the answer. I never had the patience to wait on the answer; I just spit out my request and plowed on ahead, figured I'd done my part. The rest was up to God.

The Bible tells the story of Daniel, who prayed for twenty-one days before getting an answer. As the story goes, God immediately sent Gabriel, the messenger angel with the answer. The problem was, the prince of the kingdom of Persia withstood him for twenty-one days. Even though Gabriel was dispatched immediately, the demons in charge of Persia withstood him for those three weeks. Because Daniel continued to pray, Michael, the archangel, a warrior in battle, was compelled to be put to flight and came to help Gabriel break through and deliver the answer.

I've always known that story, but never looked at it with any practical application. Accordingly, my prayer life wasn't very productive. Life is different now. I start everyday with prayer. Not just occasionally, but every day. I'm amazed at the difference it has made in my life. It doesn't mean that I always get what I want, but it has shown me that I always have what I need. God is real, and He will do for me what I can't do for myself. It starts with prayer and comes to fruition as I continue in prayer.

THERE ARE THREE ANSWERS TO PRAYER—"YES," "NOT YET," AND "I HAVE SOMETHING BETTER FOR YOU."

Prayer was difficult for me. Maybe because I went to God in prayer every time I wanted something, and especially when I needed something. It wasn't a passionate fellowship with my Creator. It wasn't a cry out for my desires. Truth be told, even when I did pray for someone else, I was probably thinking about how "I" wanted them to be healed, instead of thinking about how "they" needed to be healed. Even in prayer and repetition to God, it was about me.

Over the years, I've learned that it's not all about me. Learning that is still a work in progress. I have learned that the answers aren't always what I expect. In fact, sometimes they're miles apart, but they do tend to follow one of three scenarios. Those scenarios are—"Yes," "Not yet," and "I have something better for you." I used to think that some prayers just didn't get answered, but I've come to realize that I sometimes must meditate to see the answer to prayer. I rarely get an immediate response that is an automatic affirmation of what I want, although occasionally, that "Yes" just comes.

Too often, those "Yes" answers are the only ones I hear. The "Not yet" answers almost feel like no answer at all because I constantly want instant results. The most common answer I get from prayer though is, "I have something better for you." My ways and thoughts are never as awesome as God's ways and His thoughts. I find that, after prayer, I need to meditate and be patient because God always answers prayers! I just don't always hear the answers.

THE BIG BOOK IS THE B.S. SIFTER.
IF IT'S NOT IN THERE, IT'S PROBABLY B.S.

I struggled for years to control my drinking, yet nothing seemed to work. By the time I realized that control was hopeless, quitting was impossible. Trying to stabilize my life was exhausting. Everybody had a solution for me, but none of them worked.

Trying to act right or think right was just fleeting. Going to church, getting prayed for, being anointed with oil, and even truly believing that there was a power somewhere out there that might be able to help me still didn't work. All my thoughts and solutions, and most of everyone else's, were all B.S. They didn't get me sober.

When I was introduced to *The Big Book* of Alcoholics Anonymous, something was different. It was as if a spirit within the pages spoke to me (the Holy Spirit). It was almost like it was meant for me, like it was my story. All of it! It felt like the writer knew me. My innermost self could feel the truth of the book. I knew, without a doubt, that it was written for me and the countless number of those like me.

Being who I am, I searched for mistakes and couldn't find any. Everything I read in *The Big Book* of Alcoholics Anonymous touched my inner spirit and rang true. When it came to my sobriety, I could trust the 164 pages of basic text in *The Big Book* to be fact for me. All the solutions outside of that are questionable. *The Big Book* for me is the B.S. sifter. If it's not there, it's probably B.S.

IT'S NOT ABOUT WHAT HAPPENS TO YOU IN LIFE, IT'S HOW YOU DEAL WITH IT.

Sometimes, life is hard. Usually it's by my own making, but it's hard sometimes nonetheless. Am I ready for it? Is my toolbelt full of all the tools I've acquired from the program? Life is going to come at you from a variety of angles. You are going to experience hardships, setbacks, sorrow, and other difficulties. These things don't have any say in the outcome of your life. How you deal with these things as they come will determine your outcome in life.

If you keep a good outlook on life and are aware that there is going to be some struggles and complications from time to time, it's not so difficult. Be prepared. When life gives you lemons, make lemonade. You don't have to let what happens to you in life hold you down or hold you back. You can remain strong and continue to have progress if you deal with it head on. Your attitude will determine how you deal with it.

BRING THE BODY; THE MIND WILL FOLLOW.

For years, I thought about getting sober. Every time calamity would strike, the thought would come to the forefront of my life. "This can't keep happening," would flood my brain. I wanted so badly to stop the suffering that I was causing to myself and others. I wanted to stop going to jail and treatment and stop ending up at the brink of death. No matter how hard I thought about it, my body wouldn't cooperate.

I couldn't seem to take that action step, and I was literally going insane. In fact, insanity almost seemed like a viable option, as I figured then I'd at least be oblivious to the pain and destruction. By the grace of God, I ended up in the halls of Alcoholics Anonymous. Desperate and afraid, I decided to give one last-ditch effort to sobriety. In the meetings, I was told to go to ninety meetings in ninety days on a regular basis, so I figured I would try the same in meetings instead.

My only goal was to simply show up. As I continued for those ninety days, my mind started to clear. I started actually hearing what others shared and even began to understand. All the thinking in the world hadn't been able to change my actions, but I found that if I just showed up, if I just brought my body, my mind followed.

PRINCIPLE 2—FAITH

BOOK OF TOOLS—
THE BIG BOOK HAS ALL THE TOOLS
I NEED TO CARRY IN MY TOOLBELT.

When I was first introduced to *The Big Book* of Alcoholics Anonymous, I wasn't sure what to expect. First of all, I was told that I had to read it. I was in treatment by force, so everything I was told to do was punishment, not desire. So, during my first read-through, I figured I might learn something about alcohol and my problems with it, but I didn't hold out much hope for a solution. In fact, I didn't even notice the chapter titled, "There is a Solution."

As I stayed sober, day after day, my mind started to clear, and I started to see the things I had read in *The Big Book*. I came to realize that *The Big Book* for AA is kind of like the Bible is to the Church. Just as a Christian gets wisdom and truths from the Bible, the alcoholic gets wisdom and truths from *The Big Book* of Alcoholics Anonymous. That's not to say the two books are equal or the same! It's just to help point out the value and worth of *The Big Book* to an alcoholic in recovery.

It doesn't matter what I go through in life, *The Big Book* of Alcoholics Anonymous is my book of tools. Every bit of wisdom I hear shared seems to originate out of that book. Now when I read it, I not only see the tools that can transform my life, but I understand how to use them, not only for my own wellbeing, but also for God's purposes. Today, my toolbelt is full, so long as I have my book of tools.

AN ALCOHOLIC IS AN EGOMANIAC WITH AN INFERIORITY COMPLEX.

Talk about an oxymoron. I often drank to take away my inhibitions, all the while acting like I was all that and then some. But, why? My life sucked. Things were spiraling out of control. My life had deteriorated to the point that nothing in my life was manageable. Work, home, family, friends, all of it was completely out of my control. Did I feel insecure and inferior to others? No! I really felt like I was something, so long as I had alcohol flowing through my veins.

The truth was—being loaded masked the problem, but only for me. I became the only one who couldn't see the problem, but I had to stay drunk to keep from seeing it. Sobriety hurt too much, and drinking made the pain worse. I was screwed.

My best friend, Two Feathers, says the Lord's prayer while replacing "evil" with "ego." When I asked to deliver me from evil, I now remember, that my ego is quite possibly the biggest evil in my life that I need God to deliver me from. I am forever grateful to the members of Alcoholics Anonymous who have submitted to God's will for their lives and thus given me the tools to do the same.

PRINCIPLE 3

SURRENDER/TRUST

Trust in the Lord with all your heart, and lean not on your own understanding; in all your ways acknowledge Him, and He shall direct your paths. (Proverbs 3:5-6)

YOU HAVE TO SURRENDER TO WIN.

I'm six-and-a-half feet tall. I weigh 250 pounds, and I'm a marine. I surrender to nothing. I have been taught to NEVER surrender! Coming into Alcoholics Anonymous, I knew I had a battle to face. I had to fight hard if I wanted sobriety. I had to fight hard if I wanted to turn around all the mistakes in my life and win this battle of alcoholism. How could I surrender in the face of such a serious battle?

The problem was, this was one battle I didn't know how to fight, so I came to AA ready to learn. I was told that I must surrender to win, which was a foreign concept for me. I thought that if you surrender, you're giving up. Well, that's true, but it's exactly what I needed to do.

I had to give up trying to do this on my own power. I had to give up making my own decisions because they just weren't working. What I had to do was surrender to the fact that I am an alcoholic. I needed to surrender to Alcoholics Anonymous. I had to surrender my thoughts in order to learn a way of success in sobriety. I had to quit fighting everyone and everything. I had to surrender to win.

QUITTING WASN'T MY PROBLEM, STAYING QUIT WAS.

Quitting drinking was something I did all the time. It was easy. I'd swear it off every time I woke up with that headache. I'd stop every time I went to treatment. After all, you couldn't use in there, and I was trying to change my life. Every time I went to jail, I'd quit while I was in there. Well, most of the time. Pruno (prison wine) was pretty easy to make, and depending on who you were locked up with, it was often part of the stay.

Quitting was generally easy to do. It was staying quit that I couldn't figure out. I didn't struggle without alcohol in jail or treatment. However, the second I was out and on my own again, the cravings were overwhelming. Trying to make sense of it was fruitless. Staying quit just wasn't possible.

I genuinely liked the fellowship of like-minded people I found in bars, so those were the ones I sought out. So, why wasn't it a struggle in treatment? Maybe it's because those, too, were like-minded people, they just weren't drunk. I started going to Alcoholics Anonymous and couldn't believe what I found. I found an entire fellowship of like-minded people, who, just like me, had this obsession with alcohol. The difference was—they were sober. I felt like I was with a family where I fit in. I got comfortable there and staying quit has never been a problem since.

NOTHING CHANGES IF NOTHING CHANGES.

Sounds pretty basic and quite simple. However, over and over again, I did the same thing, expecting different results. I wasn't drinking, I wasn't stealing and lying, and I wasn't doing bad things, but things weren't getting any better. People still blamed me for all my shortcomings. No one looked at their part.

Why couldn't they notice that it was their actions that made me this way. I simply couldn't see how current things were my fault when I was doing so good. So good that my arm was getting sore from patting myself on the back. Heck, nobody else would!

As I hung around awhile, got a sponsor, and worked the steps, things really started making sense. Sure, I had stopped some bad habits, and good for that, but the changes necessary in my life weren't as simple as just stopping some specific behaviors, although, that was absolutely a necessary part.

My attitude and outlook had to change. Until I was willing to go to that extreme, nothing of any consequence changed. The correction of some bad habits and actions, while always a good idea, doesn't make my life "changed." Change comes from a spiritual overhaul of my attitude and outlook. When I face my mortality and come to the realization that I am merely a vessel in my Higher Power's will, change is simple. When I see that God can, when I can't, everything changes!

OBEDIENCE IS THE GRAVEYARD OF THE WILL.

The thing about being in charge is I get to control everything. The only thing I must be obedient to is myself, my own mind, my own desires, my own rules, and my own decisions. My, my, my, whatever I want. Self will run riot; that's what I had. Everything was based on my will. My will ended up putting me in pretty dire straits.

I had to stop running my life on my own will. I never would have survived it. *The Big Book* of Alcoholics Anonymous tells me in the steps that I should turn my will over to the care of God, a Power greater than myself that can restore me to sanity. To do that, I had to get rid of my self will. Kill it, bury it, and leave it dead.

I found that the more I surrendered to the program, the less my will mattered. It became easier to see and follow God's will for my life. It wasn't always about me. In fact, it was seldom about me. By being obedient to His will for my life, my will slowly died. I guess you could say obedience was the graveyard of my will.

THE THIRD STEP PRAYER

"God, I offer myself to Thee—to build with me and to do with me as Thou wilt. Relieve me of the bondage of self, that I may better do Thy will. Take away my difficulties, that victory over them may bear witness to those I would help of Thy Power, Thy Love, and Thy Way of life. May I do Thy will, ALWAYS!" It is not me who directs my path. I am simply a vessel for God to use if He feels so inclined.

I only offer myself to Him, not to receive power to do stuff, but to be a worthy tool that He can find use of. I ask for relief from self-centered actions, so that His will is accomplished, not mine. I ask Him to take away my difficulties, not so my life is easy, but so others will see that He is real, so they know it really works. As I change my life and it becomes a testimony to others, the victories I have are a practical witness to those I would help of God's power, love, and way of life.

This is not something that is just for today, when things go wrong, when things go right, or occasionally. I strive to do His will, ALWAYS! That's the prayer in a nutshell. I offer myself to God, I ask Him to use me for His purpose and desire, and I ask Him to get me out of myself so that I can focus on His will for me. I also ask Him to take away my difficulties in my life as a witness to others who struggle, and I ask Him to help me follow Him, ALWAYS!!!

MAN MAKES HIS PLANS, BUT GOD DIRECTS HIS STEPS.

Even my plans need God's direction, so I ask Him in my morning prayers. When I seek Him and His wisdom, I find myself content with the plans I put forward. However, if I set out to fulfill those plans on my own strength and power, I tend to fall flat on my face. No matter how hard I try, I'm just not enough on my own.

The fact is, on my own, the best I could do was find a chair in Alcoholics Anonymous. When I think about it, I'm pretty sure it was God who got me in that seat too. As I allow Him into my daily routine, I find that He directs my steps for me. I fall into far less potholes if I allow Him to be my guide.

My plans don't seem to be perfect, and I miss certain aspects of the plan due to my human nature. I'm not perfect, so neither are my plans, but God, my Higher Power, is perfect. I can rely on Him to direct my steps. He has already factored my shortcomings into the equation. So, each morning, as I map out my plans for the day, I ask God to direct my steps. Because of this, I never end up in the wrong place.

I THANK GOD, ON MY KNEES, FOR THREE THINGS EVERY MORNING— I'M ALIVE, I'M SOBER, AND I'M A MEMBER OF ALCOHOLICS ANONYMOUS.

God has become very important to me. I realize that I'm not very good at running my life. Left to my own devices, life never turned out very good. The best I could do was qualify for a chair in the halls of Alcoholics Anonymous, and I didn't even end up there on my own. I'm pretty sure there was some kind of divine intervention that went on inside of me that drove me there after I had driven myself into the ground.

Now, I'm overwhelmingly grateful to have found a place that seems to touch all the bases of my life. I'm a member of Alcoholics Anonymous, and it's because of that that I am alive. I am alive, and because of that, I get to serve God every day. I get to share what saved my life with others who are suffering the same slow, painful spiral to death.

That was once me, constantly hurting everyone around me and never having a single moment of true serenity. I was always chasing an emptiness that couldn't be filled by my hands. My heart may still have been beating, but I was dead. Today, I thank God that I'm alive, I'm sober, and I'm a member of Alcoholics Anonymous. All by the grace of God, my Higher Power.

LEAD ME NOT INTO TEMPTATION; I CAN FIND IT MYSELF.

I love this saying! It literally cracks me up. I can't say that it taught me a lot, but I appreciate it anyway. My first go-to is blame. Even now, several years into my sobriety, when something goes awry, for some reason I don't look inward first.

It is getting better, but truthfully, I still struggle. It's not out of malice or ill thought, I just immediately look out in front of myself. What happened? Who did this? Who did that? What circumstance, that I have absolutely no control of, caused this malady to come about?

Even when I look at my part, there's a moment where I almost instinctively try to figure out who led me down this path. The simple answer is nobody did. I walked the path all on my own.

Outside circumstances are not the problem in my life—I AM! When I am drinking and not living right, I submit to every temptation that comes my way. In fact, I will manufacture temptations if one doesn't show up fast enough. I do not need to be led into temptation, I can find it all by myself.

Today, I no longer look for temptations, and I no longer manufacture them. Now, I see them as the temptations they are, and when they do come, I have a wealth of experience, strength, and hope in my tool-belt to defend against them.

JESUS IS MY HIGHER POWER. ANYBODY THAT CAN TURN WATER INTO WINE IS MY KIND OF DUDE.

I cracked up when I heard this. The irony of the truth in it is just hilarious, and I need some humor in my program. I never want to take things too seriously, unless the situation absolutely calls for it. I am an alcoholic, and I seem to be drawn to other alcoholics. I relate best to people who understand me and of whom I can understand.

It seems like God has a sense of humor too. As I turn my life and will over to Him, as my Third Step suggests I should, it's quite a hilarious coincidence that I should come to realize that He can turn water into wine. Yet, His written Word tells me that I shouldn't be a drunkard, which is exactly what I am when I drink.

It's obvious to me, that God understands that some people get carried away, to say the least, when they drink. It's the fellowship with those in the program whom I actually relate to that help keep me sober, and it's nice to know I have a Higher Power that understands me too.

GOD WILL NOT GUIDE
WHERE HE DOES NOT PROVIDE.

So many things in my life didn't work out the way I had anticipated. The provisions needed to bring them to fruition were never there. I would set out on my own to make some vision a reality and something would stand in the way. Sometimes, I would hit the same one repeatedly, believing I could power through it, and the power to break through never came. Often, I'd pray for God to help me accomplish it, yet He didn't provide the miracle.

Being a strong-willed, intelligent man, it never crossed my mind that my own thoughts, my dreams, and my visions weren't enough on their own. It never dawned on me that I needed God to guide me. I always thought it was up to me to set the path, and then I simply needed to ask Him for His help. It turns out that my thoughts and my ways were the problem all along. No matter how hard I tried, God was not going to help me get somewhere He didn't want me to go.

If I wanted His provisions in my life, then I needed to seek His guidance in my life. Since choosing to seek God first, since surrendering my mornings to the Third Step Prayer, and since seeking His guidance before I set out on a mission, life has not just become manageable, but it has become successful. If God sets me on my path, there is always success to the mission because God will not guide where He does not provide.

GOD AND I ALONE DON'T ALWAYS ACHIEVE THE BEST RESULTS.

When I first heard this saying, it kind of confused me. With God, all things are possible, right? That is, until I interject my thoughts and actions into the equation. My ways have been so skewed, that I could even mess up God's plans for me. Left to my own understandings, I'm not the best member of any team.

It's not that God isn't enough. It's that I've had too much world in me and not enough Spirit. Set in my ways, sometimes God can't get through. Not due to any lack on His part, but due to much lack on mine. When I seek Him, He's always there, but His answer usually sends me to someone else. Whether that's a mentor, a church, or most often for me, a meeting of Alcoholics Anonymous. It's those I associate with that help me settle my thoughts. My Higher Power directs me to those who have conquered the issues I struggle with.

When my God shows up, it's most often in the form of another. He speaks to me through people. When I want to know what's best for me, it doesn't always just appear in my thoughts. Most often, it comes from hearing what someone else has to say, and God simply confirms it with His Spirit touching that innermost spot inside of me. I've found that, although I can do all things through Christ, He usually sends another my way to help guide me.

PRINCIPLE 3—SURRENDER/TRUST

IF I DRINK, I DIE.

It's that simple. If I drink, I die, period. Oh, it might not be instant, at least not in the physical sense. With my luck, it would be a long, drawn-out, spiritual death that kept me breathing for ages, without ever experiencing serenity. Just existing to drink in the pain, or possibly, getting drunk will send me to the dope man where I take that last hit and die a physical death from my final overdose. Maybe I'll finish off any ability at kind of relationship and die an emotional death. I'll definitely end up back at those spending issues and die a financial death.

The point is, death waits for me, hoping I'll take one more drink, giving myself over to her, but death can't have me. I've found a solution. Don't drink, period, stop, end of story. Just don't drink, and if I do that, I can actually live life. Yes, I'll still die, eventually, but not till I've accomplished what this world has set before me. I won't be that zombie, breathing but not living, just existing from day to day, hoping for it all to stop. Even welcoming death if that's what it takes for the pain to leave.

I'm done with that though. That's the me if I drink, and today, I don't drink. That means today, I won't die. Not physically, emotionally, spiritually, mentally, financially, or any otherly. It took some time and some work, but today, I don't drink, because if I do, I die.

IF *THE BIG BOOK* SAYS IT, I BELIEVE IT.

This probably sounds a bit extreme. Maybe even a bit ridiculous, but for me, it's a must. *The Big Book* of Alcoholics Anonymous has been intricate in getting me, and keeping me, sober. I trust it! But I have to trust all of it. If I can throw any part of it out, if I can discount any portion as false, wrong, or untrue, I can throw the whole thing out.

I can pick up any book based on my own knowledge and opinions. My own knowledge and opinions couldn't get me sober. I needed something that was solid and absolute, something that was the truth and worked. I found that in *The Big Book*. It has tested time and numerous afflictions of countless others.

I believe it was divinely inspired for me—the alcoholic! It addresses issues that only someone like me struggles with—the alcoholic! It provides an outline of how to overcome, how to accept, how to forgive and be forgiven, how to heal, how to succeed, and how to live life.

Not just how to get through life, but how to live it. With vision, purpose, service, faith, hope, love, patience, tolerance, and acceptance. With true joy, no matter what your life brings you through. READ THE BOOK!

F.E.A.R.—FALSE EVIDENCE APPEARING REAL

You'll never make it! You're going to amount to nothing! You'll never finish anything! You can't do it! You're not good enough, old enough, young enough, thin enough, or smart enough. Pick the adjective, I felt it all. I was in constant fear of failure, so I constantly portrayed the appearance of success, and alcohol allowed me to believe it. When I was drunk, I was on top of the world. Nothing went wrong, and if it did, I didn't notice or care. Life was great! But I couldn't stay drunk. Life kept rearing its ugly head on the few occasions that I ended up sober.

When I finally found my way to halls of Alcoholics Anonymous, acquired a sponsor, and started doing some of the work in the program, my fears started to weaken. All the things I had heard about my failures and abilities seemed like lies. Most of my fears were not founded in reality. I could make it, as long as I tried! I was going to amount to something, as long as I put in the work! I was going to finish something, as long as I followed it through! I could do it because I am good enough, old enough, young enough, thin enough, and smart enough. Pick the adjective, I feel them all. I have realized that F.E.A.R. is usually False Evidence Appearing Real, and as long as I face it all, I never have to live in it.

I'M SOBER TODAY BY THE GRACE OF GOD AND THE FELLOWSHIP OF ALCOHOLICS ANONYMOUS.

Let's take a look at Wrigley's chewing gum. Juicy Fruit was really good, but it broke down too fast. That kind of reminds me of my life. Doublemint gum, now that was my favorite! Something was different about it; it just seemed to work better and last longer. It had a flavor that set it apart, a flavor that was different and satisfied where other flavors had failed. As it turns out, Doublemint gum is the only mint that contains both spearmint and peppermint oils. The gum Doublemint had a winning combination.

That's God and AA for me. That's my Doublemint. When I gave myself to God, there wasn't a lot to give. I was a liar, a cheat, and a thief. I was broken, beat down, and hopeless. What a gem to lay at my Father's feet, saying to Him, "Here I am Lord, I give all of me to You," as if I was a gift to Him or something. His Grace took me as I was. There I was, humbled by the grace of God, yet still lost, with no idea what to do next.

Alcoholics Anonymous had been pointed out to me several times, and in desperation, I attended meetings. I didn't care what they said or what they knew. Didn't they understand that I was in a different world? How could anybody relate to me? God barely could. I kept going to meetings and became friends with some of the members. As time went on, the fellowship became comfortable. I didn't care how much they knew, till I knew how much they cared. The grace of God (my peppermint) and the fellowship of Alcoholics Anonymous (my spearmint) are my sobriety. Today, my Juicy Fruit life is over, and I enjoy my life's flavor—Doublemint.

DON'T TELL GOD YOU HAVE A BIG PROBLEM. TELL YOUR PROBLEM YOU HAVE A BIG GOD.

There is One who has all power—that One is God. How absolutely empowering it is to know that there is One more powerful than whatever comes against me or whatever I come up against. Without a doubt, that's the One I'm hitching my pony to. Think about it, a power that is ultimate. I need that every day, in one way or another.

I remember being a kid and knowing that as long as my dad was with me, I was safe. Not only was I safe, but I could attempt anything because he was there and had my back. If I came up against a problem I couldn't handle, I didn't run from it or give up. I simply introduced it to Dad and never had to worry about it again.

The Good Book says, "I can do all things through Christ my strength." I don't have to cry to God about my problem and hope He fixes it. Prayer is awesome and powerful. I can tell my problem who my God is, and nine times out of ten, my problem will give up on its own.

Most of my problems are of my own making, and I find that as I turn them over to God, He takes them away. Now, no matter how difficult something is, as I talk to God about the situation, I'm very direct in letting my problem know who my God is. When I tell my problem how big my God is, my problem suddenly seems awfully small.

I START EVERY MORNING ON MY KNEES THANKING GOD FOR THREE THINGS— I'M ALIVE, I'M SOBER, AND I'M A MEMBER OF ALCOHOLICS ANONYMOUS.

If you would have told me that, one day, my life would basically revolve around Alcoholics Anonymous, I would have told you that you were crazy, yet today, that's exactly how I live. Even more than that, I absolutely love it. Life today couldn't be better.

I could have more money, or a bigger house, or even less stress, which is almost impossible in today's world, but life itself is so awesome today that I can't even fathom it being any better. I'm alive, which not so many years ago, I didn't think I would be at sixty-five.

The life I was living was heading me straight to death on a fast track. I'm sober which was never in the plans for me. I was so deeply entrenched in my alcoholism that any way out was seemingly impossible. Both of those, being alive and being sober, are a direct result of joining Alcoholics Anonymous.

Through the whole program of Alcoholics Anonymous, getting a sponsor, working the steps, and leaning on and turning to a Higher Power, I was able to get sober. Upon getting sober, life started to change, death seemed distant, and I suddenly felt alive.

My prayers are many, and sometimes often, but first and foremost, I thank God that I'm alive, I'm sober, and I'm a member of Alcoholics Anonymous.

BUT FOR THE GRACE OF GOD.

I'm one of the lucky ones! I like to think that I should get the credit for my life being OK now. After all, I'm the one that stopped drinking, I'm the one that went to the meetings, I read the literature, I did the service work, I got a sponsor, I accepted sponsees, I got involved with the steering committee and the board of our fellowship hall, I joined clean and sober bowling, and I even joined the clean and sober softball association. In all, I have done a lot of work to get to where I am.

The truth is that I'm one of the lucky ones. I'm glad life isn't fair. If it was, the price I would have to pay for the life I had lived and the things I had done would never have allowed me the opportunity for the life I have now.

It was the grace of God that got me into Alcoholics Anonymous. It was Alcoholics Anonymous that taught me faith without works is dead. So, all that work I talked about that "I" did, was only possible by the grace of God that got me into the program that could change my life.

As I look back over my sobriety, it's clear to see that it was His grace that carried me through a multitude of my issues. If not for the grace of God, my life would be over.

ISM—I SPONSOR MYSELF.

ISM is the major problem with alcoholism. Alcohol is kind of like guns. In and of themselves, they're nothing. They sit there doing no good, nor bad; they just are. It's the hands they end up in that makes the difference.

If a competition shooter or a hunter uses his guns for those purposes, the gun causes no problem. If a soldier or police officer are acting appropriately, the gun is not problematic; instead it is helpful. However, in the hands of someone with criminal tendencies, the gun can destroy lives, not only the criminals, but their families, friends, and everyone they acted out towards.

Alcohol in the hands of a non-alcoholic causes no problem, whether it's a toast at an event, a glass of wine with dinner, or communion at church. However, alcohol is a major problem for me and poses a threat to my life. Not because of the alcohol, but because of the ISM.

When I'm in the throes of alcohol use, I am not getting help from others. I'm stuck in my ISM, which means, "I Sponsor Myself." That's what got me here in the first place. It's important that I understand my alcoholism, get help from others, and do away with the ISM.

A PROBLEM SHARED IS A PROBLEM HALVED.

When trouble comes my way, when I have problems that weigh me down, sometimes life is almost too much to bear. Handling all the pressures of life is hard for one person to cope with. Having a wife has helped me through the more difficult times. With someone to shoulder the burdens with me, some of the weight of the situation is lifted, which makes the burdens seem smaller. The fact is, when I share any problem with another, they tend to carry part of the load for me.

Getting sober was one of the hardest things I ever tried to do in my life. I failed miserably, no matter how much effort I put into it. It was too big to handle on my own. When I came into Alcoholics Anonymous, I noticed that almost everything said "We."—"We admitted" or "We choose"—or following the principles could restore "us," turn "our" will, and so on. The burdens were shared by a collective group. Although my problems were personal to me, the solution was shared by the fellowship.

Everyone who had suffered as I had been suffering seemed to understand that they couldn't do it on their own. They also seemed to believe that they couldn't keep it to themselves if they didn't give it away to others. I may have created the destruction of my life myself, but I didn't have to claw my way back alone. There was a multitude of people in the fellowship ready, willing, and able to help me with my situation. They all knew that a problem shared is a problem halved and taught that to me. The load I carried became lighter, and the burden became tolerable as I shared my problems with others. The heaviness of the weight was literally cut in half.

EGO—EDGING GOD OUT

I was told that I had an ego, and I was told to lose it. My ego was all I had left, even though in my shape, I had nothing to be egotistical about. Running on my ego got me a messed-up life, but it was mine, and I was holding onto it. It was up to me to change my life. Without my ego, how would I have the power to succeed in actually changing my life? There was my problem.

Although my best decisions ended me up in a chair at Alcoholics Anonymous, I still felt I was my best bet. It was up to me to do this. The problem was, try as I might, I couldn't. In the literature of *The Big Book*, I learned I wasn't meant to run my own life. I was to turn my will, and my life, over to the care of God as I understood Him. My ego was causing me to edge God out. I was contemplating my own decisions based solely on my own desires, my own feelings, and my own knowledge. Asking God what to do, seeking His advice, didn't seem like taking action to me.

It's actually quite the opposite. As I continued to read the literature, and work the steps, I found that, through prayer and meditation, I could improve my conscious contact with God and receive knowledge of His will for me and the power to carry it out. It was my ego that was stopping me from being the person I was created to be. Who better to show me that than He who created me. I was sick and tired of being sick and tired, and I had to quit edging God out if I wanted to become a sober, productive member of society. It was His guidance I needed, not my own.

PRINCIPLE 3—SURRENDER/TRUST

AA IS MY FAMILY, MY SCHOOL, AND MY CHURCH.

I love my church. I'm actually the recovery pastor there, and they give me free rein to run recovery meetings, so we have quite a few. I also love my family. I have seven children, twenty-three grandchildren, and two great-grandchildren. It's a ton of work, but a joy I'm glad to experience. However, those are both individual "entities." Although they are a big part of my life, they wouldn't exist in my world if I hadn't found Alcoholics Anonymous. So, I take nothing away from the importance of either one of them when I say that AA is my family, my school, and my church. I have a fellowship in Alcoholics Anonymous that I rely on, in the same fashion as I rely on my family. In some aspects, I rely on it more. The people in recovery understand things that actual family members just can't because they didn't share the malady I share with the fellowship. The things I learn in AA can't be taught in a school. They are life lived experiences that only someone with my disease could explain or comprehend. Maybe it's the brutal honesty that is demanded in the halls of AA, which doesn't seem to be preached in the same way at a church, that makes God so huge to us. When we get delivered from our past, we know it couldn't be of our own doing.

We were hopeless when we got here, and our steps lead us to a God that does for us what we can't do for ourselves. Sometimes, it seems like churches want us to just accept God, and we can't because we're too dirty. It takes a process that my family of AA members can teach me in the school of Alcoholics Anonymous. That process guides me to a Higher Power, which then encompasses my entire being. AA truly is my family, my school, and my church.

THOUGHTS THAT KEEP ME SOBER

PRINCIPLE 4

HONESTY

For I say, through the grace given to me, to everyone who is among you, not to think of himself more highly than he ought to think, but to think soberly, as God has dealt to each one a measure of faith. (Romans 12:3)

YOU ONLY HAVE TO CHANGE ONE THING—EVERYTHING!

Everything? Really? How is that even possible? Living in my addictions, all my decisions were based on protecting that life. A life full of self-centered thoughts and actions to protect my ability to drink or drug as I so desired, despite the consequences to myself or damage to others. Everything in my life worked together toward that goal. It wasn't planned or thought out, it just was.

I don't quite know how it got that way, but the fact is, that's how it was. Everything was a mess, and the thought of fixing it was overwhelming. No way could I accomplish such a task. Maybe this thing, or that thing, but not everything. Nonetheless, I couldn't stay where I was, and I had to do something. The best I could do was commit myself to getting a sponsor and try my best to follow their suggestions.

Little-by-little, bit-by-bit, my life started to change. Each shortcoming that fell away gave me strength to attack another. Usually, it wasn't even a fight. Simply living out the suggestions from my sponsor seemed to cause issues to evaporate, vanishing into thin air and disappearing altogether. Changing everything was like staying sober forever. It wasn't comprehendible, but changing what I can for today is like staying sober one day at a time. As I worked on what I could, constantly making those little changes I was capable of, life progressed. When I look at how I live today, compared to how I lived in my addictions, everything has changed.

MONEY WON'T MAKE YOU HAPPY, AND WORK WON'T MAKE YOU FULFILLED.

We have all heard the saying, "Money can't buy happiness," but to those of us who never had any, we don't buy it. Even if money couldn't buy happiness, it's bound to make misery more tolerable. Yet, we see celebrities and sports figures loaded with cash still living unsatisfied lives.

What we aspire to achieve doesn't seem to provide the joy we seek. I think that's the key for me—joy! It's not really the happiness I desire, it's joy. Happiness is fleeting, it comes and goes, and is simply a feeling based on circumstances. Joy, on the other hand, is an attitude that defies circumstances.

I have spent the better half of my life working and working hard. I like the sense of accomplishment that it gives me. However, no matter how hard or long I work, I never end up truly fulfilled, at least not from the work.

When I do service, something happens. It doesn't even seem like work. It gets me out of myself, and while I'm serving others, my issues don't exist. I did not create me, my Higher Power, God, did. He knows what He created me for, and that was certainly not to fulfill myself. The example I am given by God, my Higher Power, is to give ALL of myself to the service of others, to the point of death. That's what He did!

Seeking money and working till my fingers bled never made me happy and fulfilled. I was just tired and confused. Seeking what God's plan for me was, and seeking to help others in their needs, has given me joy I never imagined. Wealth and success don't buy happiness and fulfillment, but following my Higher Power gives me the joy of both.

NORMAL PEOPLE CHANGE THEIR BEHAVIOR TO ACCOMMODATE THEIR GOAL. ALCOHOLICS CHANGE THEIR GOAL TO ACCOMMODATE THEIR BEHAVIOR.

The truth in that puts an exclamation point on my being an alcoholic. Most of my life, if my behaviors didn't line up with my goal, I'd simply change my goal. I enjoyed my actions and wasn't about to change them. My life was of my making, and nobody was going to tell me what to do. If the standards I was living kept me from progressing the way I should, I'd just lower my standards.

Slowly but surely, my life was deteriorating. Goals had become wishes, and hope was fleeting. Suddenly, I realized that my life was deteriorating faster than I could lower my standards. I was stuck in a downward spiral, just waiting for it all to end.

By the grace of God, I found myself in the halls of Alcoholics Anonymous. A gentleman that was far from normal told me that I was sicker than I realized. That was quite a statement, since I already believed that I was as sick as one could be. He told me that he was going to be my sponsor and that I was going to follow his suggestions.

I thank God for that man every day. I believe that was the real start of my return to sanity. He taught me that I can't think myself into a new way of living, but I can live my way into a new way of thinking. I guess another way of looking at that is this: I can't change my goal to accommodate my behavior, but I have to change my behavior to accommodate my goal. It hasn't made me normal, and I'm actually glad about that, because I like who I am today. It has made me capable of looking at situations and understanding when it's my behavior that needs to change. It has also given me the ability to teach others, which gives me a life worth living.

YOU CAN'T CHASE HAPPINESS, YOU HAVE TO FIND IT WHERE YOU ARE.

Actually, you can chase happiness, but you will never find it that way. Happiness isn't something that's just out there, waiting for me to come and find it. Happiness comes from within me. Circumstances can definitely affect my happiness, but they don't have to regulate it.

My attitude and outlook upon life determines my happiness. Life doesn't always go my way. Quite often, the results I'm shooting for don't exactly solidify. Sometimes, I am way off. Setbacks, while challenging, don't have to steal my joy away and leave me unhappy. My happiness comes from a process of life, and an overwhelming outlook that I am not the end of all existence.

I know that there is a Power greater than myself that guides me. My sanity isn't stifled by my own limitations. God created me, and therefore He is the best source of my happiness.

On a regular basis, we see pro athletes, movie stars, business moguls, and the like, seeming with the world by the tail, lacking happiness and ending up with depleted lives because of it. To me, that's proof positive that outside conditions don't produce happiness. They may affect the degree of happiness in a minor way, but the happiness that surpasses all understanding can only come from within, and only from our Creator.

SERIOUS THINKING OR SLOPPY THINKING?

Do my thoughts match up with reality? Are my dreams achievable or are they unrealistic thoughts that don't line up with any conceivable course of action? There's nothing wrong with having dreams and desires. I suppose it doesn't even hurt if some of those thoughts involve impossibilities, so long as I understand that.

There is a difference though between serious thinking and sloppy thinking. One sets me on a selfish path, with no quality in sight at its end result, and the other sets me on a path with success at its finish line.

Sloppy thinking lacks care, both for myself and others. The end result doesn't matter because the immediate pleasure is my goal. It takes little thought as contemplating the consequence to the action isn't part of the equation. As far as effort, there isn't any. Sloppy thinking doesn't afford for any kind of work on a plan. The effort is minimal, so moving on the goal is quick and easy.

On the other hand, serious thinking is generally a quest for what is true. When I have a serious thought, I'm thinking about the realities of life. I think about the outcome of the action when it reaches the finale. Serious thinking involves my understanding as opposed to my casual thought. Life is going to move forward, and my mind is going to continue to process. How that works out for me will depend on whether I apply serious or sloppy thinking

YOU ARE AS SICK AS YOUR SECRETS.

I guess I was one sick puppy. I had secrets I was keeping from myself. Nobody knew what I was really all about. People only saw whatever part of me I wanted them to see. Work didn't know what I was like at home, and the church didn't know what I was like when I was out in the town. One friend would know a part of me, while another would know something else. Nobody knew all of me, and I survived this way for years. It was part of my self-preservation.

The truth is—most of my secrets weren't secrets at all. I have come to find that pretty much everyone knew what I was all about. It got to the point where the only one I was fooling was myself. I'm the one who was being hurt by it. That didn't change when I tried to get sober. If I went to meetings, met some friends, and played the part, nobody would know if I was being honest. It couldn't hurt to drink occasionally, as long as no one knew. It couldn't hurt to go to the casino when I'm supposed to be at work, as long as no one knew.

That had been the issue all along. I couldn't be honest to anyone, including myself. My whole life was a secret. The problem was, I knew it! I knew I wasn't honest; I knew I was deceitful. After I stopped drinking, I found I couldn't get better with secrets. They always came back to haunt me when I took inventory. They were keeping me from achieving a point of surrender where I could work an honest program. I knew I couldn't stay sober this way. I wanted to be well, so today, I have no secrets, well ... not that many.

WHAT I DEAL WITH EVERY DAY IS UNRESOLVED ALCOHOLISM.

Just because I don't drink doesn't mean I'm not an alcoholic. I may have overcome the obsession to open the bottle and pour it down my throat, but alcoholism is a lifelong disease. I am simply granted a daily reprieve contingent on my spiritual condition. If I let down my guard, if I allow my spiritual health to deteriorate, my alcoholism will rear its ugly head and try to help me out. That's right, my disease will tell me it's not a problem, it's a solution.

Each and every day, I wake up as an alcoholic. Whether I dwell on that, or dwell on a joyous life, is up to me. Make no mistake about it though, my alcoholism always wants to win that thought over, However, my Higher Power is more powerful than my alcoholism.

I'm told in, "How It Works," that there is One who has all power. When I get up and seek Him first, the alcoholism is suppressed immediately. Throughout the day, it may try and come back, but I've been taught how to resolve that. I have literature to turn to, friends I can call, and meetings I can go to.

With God, my Higher Power, I'm never alone anyway, and He can win any battle I struggle with. Resolving my issues becomes constant with His help, so if I'm going to deal with unresolved alcoholism on a daily basis, I'm going to simply work the program of Alcoholics Anonymous on a daily basis. The solution is far more powerful than the problem.

TO THINE OWN SELF BE TRUE.

I have come to realize that I can't please all the people I want to at the same time. That being so, why do I still try to? It's not something I consciously do, but one by one, as I encounter people and situations, I want to be accepted and liked. People have differing opinions and beliefs, and you can be friends with any or all of them, but you can't be true to them all.

You can be truthful and honest, but your beliefs will only line up with some of them. Every coin I've received each year has, "To thine own self be true," circling the coin. I never paid that much attention to it, until I had differing opinions from two people whose opinions I trusted.

When I heard someone at a meeting say, "To thine own self be true," it stirred something inside of me. I needed to be true to myself. Whichever friend's opinion lined up with my beliefs, that's the one I would go with. Only God and I know the absolute truth about my life, my opinions, and my beliefs. In knowing myself, I must be true to myself in all things.

Secrets may fool some, but I will always know how my life lines up with my beliefs. It affects my attitude if I try lying to myself because I know when I'm doing it. I must always be true to myself, no matter what. It is my beliefs and how well I stay true to them that enables me to draw from my Higher Power and know that I have integrity.

THE LEAST HAPPY SOUL IS THE SOUL THAT DOESN'T KNOW IT'S NOT HAPPY.

I didn't figure this one out till I had been sober a minute. You see, I didn't know I was devoid of happiness for a long time. For quite a while, life seemed fun. Everything I did, everywhere I went, I was the life of the party. Happiness surrounded me.

Then I would sober up, take a good look at my life, and go right back to the thing that covered the crud— alcohol. After that came the happiness again. All the pains of life disappeared as the magic elixir coated my senses. I truly thought it brought happiness to my life, when in reality, it just covered up the issues, but only temporarily.

Every time the alcohol wore off, so did the happiness. It got to the point where I couldn't even drink in the happiness. It quit working. Through several circumstances, I ended up in the halls of Alcoholics Anonymous. Over time, as my head began to clear, I started to see things in a new light. The happiness I saw in the halls was real, not manufactured, like mine had been.

I found myself desperately wanting what they had. A happiness that wasn't regulated by external circumstances. A happiness that came from deep inside their very soul. For the first time, I understood what happiness was. It was a choice, regardless of issues.

Happiness fills my life today because I choose to be filled with it. I let it engulf me instead of trying to make it come to me. Today, as I look back over my life, it's extremely clear that the least happy my soul ever was, was when I didn't know I wasn't happy. That was when I was truly lost, and sobriety changed that.

FIRST I'D TAKE A DRINK,
THEN THE DRINK WOULD TAKE ME.

This is the power alcohol has over me if I drink. Once I have one, I lose control, and I don't know what's going to happen after that. If I choose to take a drink, that drink will take me anywhere it wants to. I could go home. I could go to the dope house. I could go looking for chicks. I could just stay in the bar until I pass out, or I could get taken to jail for trying to drive home.

Whatever the choice, I have no control over it. All rational thought is gone. Logic does not exist. For me, having one or two has become having one drink or not leaving till 2:00 in the morning. I never know which one, but home is not usually where I end up. The only way I can have any power over alcohol is to make sure I don't touch it. If I don't take a drink, it can't take me!

IF I DRINK, THERE WILL BE NO FRUIT TO BEAR FROM THIS BROKEN TREE.

God is so good! I came into Alcoholics Anonymous as broken as one man could be. I had no purpose and very little, if any, worth. My value as a productive member of society was non-existent. I was like a broken tree, incapable of bearing fruit. Hopeless doesn't do it justice, but I'm not sure what's below that. I only know that's where I was.

It's said, "By your fruits, they will know you," and whether it was family, friends, court, jails, treatment centers, and anything or anyone else, they knew me, and all the fruit was rotten. Nothing grew on this tree anymore.

Alcoholics Anonymous has proven to be the fertilizer, and the members have been the gardeners. The wisdom I hear in the meetings prunes me, and the program causes the breaks to mend and my tree of life to grow.

My Higher Power, whom I choose to call God, has delivered me from the destruction of my own selfish tendencies. There are actually some blossoms on this tree on a regular basis. Fruit has started to pop up on the branches.

As long as I stay sober, my tree of life stays healthy. I need to keep it fertilized, and I need to keep it pruned. In other words, I need to live in the program of Alcoholics Anonymous, and I need to stay in the fellowship of the members. If I do that, I won't break, but if I drink, there will be no fruit to bear from this broken tree.

DRINKING TO SHOW SOMEBODY IS LIKE DRINKING POISON AND EXPECTING THE OTHER PERSON TO DIE.

I can't even count the number of times I've told my wife, "I'll show you," and then went and got hammered. Like, "This will fix her." It was me that ended up without a car after wrecking it. It was me who ended up broke. It was me who ended up behind bars, locked up again, "Cause I was going to show her."

We may hurt or annoy the other person when we do this, but it's ourselves that truly suffer by having to pay the consequences. It's our life that spirals downhill, ever close to extinction. All hope in doing anything for the betterment of our lives are gone when we try to hurt someone else by doing something damaging to ourselves. When I drink to, "show her," or "show somebody else," it truly is like drinking poison and expecting the other person to die. Absolute madness, it's crazy!

IF YOU CAN'T REMEMBER YOUR LAST DRINK, YOU PROBABLY HAVEN'T HAD IT YET.

I came in and out of Alcoholics Anonymous several times in my attempt to live a clean and sober life. Whenever I was asked for my AA birthday, I didn't remember it. I just knew that I didn't want to drink anymore, so I started going to meetings. The actual day I quit didn't matter to me. Just the fact that I wasn't drinking that particular day was enough for me. I usually couldn't even remember exactly when I had my last drink. I never really saw any importance to it. Of course, I kept getting drunk.

One thing is for sure, since I quit drinking with a real measure of success, I've never forgotten my last drink. I will never forget that last time I was loaded. I'll never forget my first day of sobriety, and my AA birthday is forever etched into my brain. Maybe there's something to it. I guess my last one set such an impression on me that I couldn't forget it. At least I know, I haven't had a drink since. There have been several times that the simple desire to not lose my sober date has made me think twice about relapsing. My last time drinking, and remembering that date, helps to insure me that I've had my last drink.

CLEAR CONSCIENCE

A friend of mine always sums up his walk in sobriety with two words—clean conscience. I've grabbed onto that thought because of the logical sense it makes. Whether I've wanted to accept it or not, there has always been a God-conscience-meter inside me. When I do something wrong, I know it. If I treat my wife poorly, if I cut someone off in traffic, if I call in sick when I'm really feeling fine, if I do something I'm not supposed to, or if I don't do something I'm supposed to do, I know it.

I'm not talking about accidental mistakes or things I don't recognize. I'm sure I've cut people off in traffic without realizing it, but that's not what I'm referring to. When I knowingly lie, cheat, or steal, my conscience is quite aware of it. I can't help but feel it deep within me. It's almost as if my soul suffers.

The idea of a clean conscience was relatively foreign to me prior to hearing it spoken out loud, but since then, it has become intriguing. If I live life appropriately, it's not such a strange concept. If I strive to do the right thing, if I stray away from lying, cheating, and stealing, a clean conscience is the result. I wouldn't say that I necessarily sum up my sobriety with just those two words, but I will say that a clean conscience certainly sums up a perfect day in recovery.

IF YOU'RE IN YOUR MIND, YOU'RE BEHIND ENEMY LINES.

I've always said, "If I'm in my mind, I'm in a bad neighborhood," but saying behind enemy lines really puts an exclamation point on it. See, if I'm in a bad neighborhood, I can simply leave the neighborhood I'm in and go somewhere else, which I do have to do from time to time. Trust me, my head is not a good neighborhood to hang out in. However, when I think of being behind enemy lines, I would have most likely been killed.

My disease gives me a mental obsession to drink, and the truth is, it wants to kill me. It will use my mind against me if it gets the chance, if I give it the chance, and that's exactly what I must remember. I must stay out of my mind and in service, that's what it comes down to. Being of service to others, helping others, fellowshipping with others, and every other thing I've learned in the halls of Alcoholics Anonymous helps to keep me out of my mind.

Working a program where I understand that I can't do it myself, and that it's dangerous, even deadly, to try, works. Thoughts from my mind being helped along by my alcoholism got me to AA. Then, AA taught me to keep it simple and stay out of my mind.

CHARACTER IS DOING THE RIGHT THING WHEN NOBODY ELSE KNOWS IT.

When somebody is around me, and can see what I'm doing, it's not so hard to do the right thing. I don't want people to see me acting like a jerk. I don't want them to see me being a liar, a cheat, or a thief. I don't want them to see me be inconsiderate, rude, or anything negative. I want them to see me at my best. I want their acceptance and respect.

None of that has anything to do with character. Anyone, regardless of his or her character, can suck it up enough to do the right thing when someone else is around. We can even teach monkeys to do that, but what about when nobody is watching? What if no one will see or nobody will ever know? Do you do the right thing then? That's where the real test of character comes in.

I believe, if you truly do what's right, especially when nobody else knows, your character will automatically shine forth around others as well. Do I give back the money when I receive too much change? Do I cheat on my taxes? Do I help when asked, or do I make up some excuse and lie? Character is doing the right thing when nobody else knows it. Only you will know, in the secret places, what your character really is. However, your character, in the places nobody else knows, will show forth in your daily life, so always be of good character.

IF YOU TELL THE TRUTH, IT BECOMES YOUR PAST. IF YOU TELL A LIE, IT BECOMES YOUR FUTURE.

One of the things we are called to do is be absolutely honest. Sometimes, this is hard, and after living in lies for so long, we often are not sure what the truth really is. This is partly because the lies of our past are now being lived out in our present. This might be because we are holding onto things that eat at us, or it could be because of the groundwork we laid out with the lies we have portrayed our life to be. The words we speak can set things in motion, and if the truth isn't told, proper motions are missed.

The direction we put our lives in is not based on truth, so the prospect of success is greatly reduced. Just like the results we receive when we do our Fourth and Fifth Steps, when we are honest, all the crud becomes a part of our past. It becomes something we can let go of and move forward from. When we are dishonest and lie, we carry that with us, as it still exists in our lives. We just buried it to be dug up later, either by ourselves or by someone else.

I think this is a big part of where our "yets" come from. They are things we're holding onto because we haven't been truthful about them. Be honest about everything and your defects of character will leave. Lie and those shortcomings will surface again and again.

ALCOHOLICS ARE PEOPLE WHO BELIEVE THE WHOLE WORLD IS AGAINST THEM, AND THEY WOULDN'T HAVE IT ANY OTHER WAY.

I swear it seems like we alcoholics love pain. Maybe it's not so much that we love it, we just seem compatible with it. Change can be scary and difficult. Sometimes, the familiar, no matter how much it hurts, is easier than changing. We seem to find some sick kind of acceptance of ourselves if we're all that we have. "Poor me, poor me, pour me a drink."

How easy it is to just keep drinking as long as we feel this way. We want to be free of the alcohol, but it's ravishing. We want to be free of the obsession, but we really don't want to give up the comforts that drinking provides, even though it's been years since it provided any comforts. The belief that the entire world is against us, allows us to keep from looking at our own actions, our own attitudes, our own behaviors, and our own lives. We've learned how to live this way, and we embrace it as a fact.

The truth is the world is not against us. We have a disease that is against us, and it will wreak havoc on us every chance it gets. Once we come to realize that we can accept help from others and trust that they are not all out to get us, change will come on its own. Just surrender, you are really only fighting yourself.

IT ALWAYS GETS WORSE;
IT NEVER GETS BETTER
(IF YOU CONTINUE TO DRINK).

I wanted to learn how to control my drinking. I wanted the pain and suffering, both what I felt and what I caused to others, to stop. I wanted life to get better, but no matter how hard I tried, it always got worse. I prayed. I hoped. I went to treatment, and even jail, but try as I might, each time I drank again, it was never a better outcome. It was always the same destructive result.

When I came into Alcoholics Anonymous, I was told it would always get worse. It would never get better. I was also told that I never had to drink again, even if I wanted to. That was the solution. If I just don't drink, it can't get worse. That brought a whole new problem to me. How do I not drink?

I had no idea how to accomplish that, but the people in the halls of Alcoholics Anonymous seemed to have figured it out. As I listened to them, I found they were just like me, only sober. If their lives and their experiences had been the same as what I was dealing with, and they had found a solution, then I could too.

I joined Alcoholics Anonymous and followed their suggestions to the best of my ability. Life gets better and better and will never get worse again, as long as I stay in the fellowship and do not drink.

ALCOHOL WAS NOT MY PROBLEM; IT WAS MY SOLUTION.

I've heard people say that alcohol never did anything for them. I can't say that. Alcohol wasn't my enemy, or at least it didn't seem like it. It was my friend. Alcohol was never my problem. Alcohol was my solution to everything. If work was particularly stressful, a few drinks washed away the stress. If my day had been overly busy, alcohol brought instant relaxation. When someone or something nagged at my life, I could drink away the noise and silence the irritation. On great days, a little bit of partying was in order. When you win the game, get the promotion, meet the new mate, or any positive uplifting event occurs, who doesn't toss down a few cold ones in vibrant celebration. You see, alcohol wasn't my problem, it was my solution, for everything.

Here's the problem, it quit working. At that point, I was stuck. My solution to life didn't work anymore, and I came face-to-face with the real problem—ME! Instead of facing life daily and dealing with my issues, I had been stuffing them and stacking them till the alcohol just couldn't hold up the pile any longer. When everything came crashing down under the weight of my life, I'm grateful I found the program of Alcoholics Anonymous. It was there that I discovered the solution to my real problem—me.

IT'S NOT JUST WHAT ALCOHOL DOES TO ME; IT'S WHERE IT TAKES ME.

It's bad enough what alcohol does to me. It affects my relationships as it turns me into a complete jerk. It affects my job as my work ethic isn't as important as my next fix. It affects my freedom to do what I'd like as I'm physically incapable of handling even mental tasks, let alone drive or such. It affects my ability to have any real, true rational thought, making it impossible to control my decisions.

Where it takes me is something else altogether because I have no real, true rational thought and anything goes. I don't know if I'll end up at the crack house, at the bar when it's closing time, caught up in a fight, any other type of illegal action, or even with someone who isn't my wife. Once I touch alcohol, ALL BETS ARE OFF! I have no control over what I'll choose to do, who I'll choose to do it with, or where I'll choose to do it. Alcohol takes me places I do not want to go.

ALCOHOLIC—IF YOU GET RID OF THE ALCOHOL, YOU'RE STILL STUCK WITH THE IC.

If you sober up a drunk horse thief, what are you left with? A sober horse thief, plain and simple. Alcohol wasn't my problem, it was my solution, but at some point, it quit working for me. The problems had become too much, and they got so bad that not even alcohol or drugs could make it seem better. I knew I was in trouble, but I couldn't stop. If only I could put down the bottle long enough to gain some clarity, but I couldn't. I was so stuck, that no issue or problem could be addressed due to my constant inebriation.

After treatment several times, joining AA, and getting a sponsor, I was able to quit drinking for a period. At first, I wasn't even sure if I liked it. I felt everything, because everything was still there, everything except the alcohol. Without my numbing agent, alcohol, I had nothing to take the bad feelings away.

Stopping drinking, by itself, did make life better, to a degree, but getting rid of the alcohol didn't get rid of the IC. I am still an alcoholic, and if I don't work some type of program for the welfare of my sobriety, my life sober will end up as icky as my life drunk. I need to do the work, and if I do, I can be assured that the IC will go away.

THOUGHTS THAT KEEP ME SOBER

PRINCIPLE 5

COURAGE

For God has not given us a spirit of fear, but of power and of love and of a sound mind.
(2 Timothy 1:7)

YOU CAN'T FIX THE PROBLEMS YOU'VE CREATED WITH THE SAME THINKING THAT CREATED THEM.

Coming into Alcoholics Anonymous did far more for me than just teach me how to stay sober. Don't get me wrong, if I hadn't gotten sober, it couldn't have done anything else for me, but upon getting sober, endless possibilities started to reveal themselves.

I was told I had stinking thinking, which basically meant I didn't know, or understand, how my mind plays tricks on me. Coupled with my physical addiction, the mental obsession constantly wanted to drive me back to my drink. The alcohol settled those pains, if only I could control it. The problem was, I couldn't.

I had come to realize that, left the way I was, I was hopeless. In Alcoholics Anonymous, I was taught to change my thinking. I had to come to terms with the fact that alcohol and I were not meant to be together. I couldn't think my way into sobriety, so every time alcohol came into the forefront of my mind, I simply threw the thought out of my head. As I continued to go to meetings, I was taught new ways of thinking.

I learned that I needed guidance from a Power greater than myself. Some power or entity that could shape new thoughts. Something that could actually help me formulate appropriate thoughts. God knows I couldn't do that myself. I used to think alcohol solved problems, but now I realize, it only postpones them and creates new ones. Today, my problems are small and few as I've learned to let God, and the program of Alcoholics Anonymous, guide my thinking, instead of my own selfish desires.

PRINCIPLE 5—COURAGE

YOU CAN'T THINK YOURSELF INTO A NEW WAY OF LIVING; YOU HAVE TO LIVE YOURSELF INTO A NEW WAY OF THINKING.

For years I wanted to quit drinking. I thought of how life would be if I wasn't constantly drunk. I would tell myself things like, "Tomorrow I'm not going to drink," or "I'm just going to have one or two," or any other series of things that could really change my life.

I would think about spending more time with my wife, my kids, or my grandkids, I would think about working more. The problem was, every day, I ended up drunk, and not one of those things happened. No matter how much I would think about it, my life wouldn't change. I just couldn't think myself into a new way of living, no matter how hard I tried.

When I heard this saying telling me that I had to live myself into a new way of thinking, something clicked. I guess I realized … until I quit drinking, all the thinking in the world wasn't going to change the way I was living.

Once I sobered up, I started to live differently. The unmanageability of my life started to lighten, rational thought came back, and I wasn't such a liar, cheat, and thief anymore. The better I tried to live my life, the clearer my mind worked. I found it to be absolutely true—I couldn't think myself into a new way of living, I had to live myself into a new way of thinking.

YOU ONLY GET OUT OF IT
WHAT YOU PUT INTO IT.

A little bit of effort usually produces a little bit of results, right? It would make sense then, that a lot of effort would produce a lot of results. Sounds pretty simple. By the time I was ready to get sober, my life was a mess. I had put years of effort into screwing it up, without even realizing that was what I was doing.

Drinking was a daily event. It was just a part of my life. It wasn't something I thought about, it was just something I did, every day, so I needed a solution that was a daily event. Without really realizing it, I had put a lot of effort into my alcoholism, so it made sense that it would take a lot of effort to break away from that addiction.

Since I had worked on being drunk every day, I would have to work on being sober every day with just as much vigor. Alcoholics Anonymous introduced me to a program that was simple, but not necessarily easy. It was going to take some serious work.

The more effort I put into my sobriety (meetings, working with others, doing service work, etc.), the more I seemed to get out of life. After doing the work on a daily basis, day after day, it has become a lifestyle. I have gotten out of sobriety just as much as I put into it. But that's only by doing the work. I actually believe that you not only get out of it what you put into it, but you get more as it multiplies with your service.

YOUR PROBLEM MAY HAVE MY NAME ON IT, BUT THE SOLUTION HAS YOUR NAME ON IT.

So often, I want to blame my problem on someone else. After all, sometimes it really seems like I'm the innocent party. Even if my problem is the result of someone else's actions, that fact does nothing to help the situation. Once it's there, it really doesn't matter where the problem came from.

The question is, "What can be done to fix it or change it?" If I sit around waiting for someone else to make it right, nothing may happen. If I can take ownership of the problem, I can facilitate a change to it. Life is work, and if I don't work at it, I become a victim by choice.

By owning the problem, it becomes possible for me to do the work necessary to fix it. Nobody was put in this world to solve my problems. People everywhere are overcome with situations that create problems in their lives, some not by their own doing, but it's our responsibility to ourselves to do something about it. The solution has our name on it! No matter where the problem came from.

PRAY LIKE IT DEPENDS ON HIM.
WORK LIKE IT DEPENDS ON YOU.

I love this. Many times, I've prayed, and then sat back and done nothing, waiting for God's response. Patiently, and more often not so patiently, I have wondered where the answer was. Or I questioned if my prayer wasn't sincere enough, or long enough, or if it was too long and pompous. I often asked, "Where is that miracle answer that's going to transform my life or the life of the one I'm praying for?" I would pray genuinely believing that it all depends on God, not me.

I have two books that I absolutely believe in. My life is guided by them. One is the Bible, the inspired Word of God. The other is *The Big Book* of Alcoholics Anonymous. I feel it is also an inspired word from God for those who have the malady I carry. I believe that wholly. Both books tell me that faith without works is dead. So, praying, even with faith that could move a mountain, is futile if I don't do my part.

Sometimes, I'm not capable of certain things, and our promises tell us that God will do for us what we can't do for ourselves. However, if there's some part that I need to take care of, the answer won't surface if I don't take care of it. I know it's His grace, not my works, that really produce the results, but my faithfulness is acted out in my acceptance of that work. Life is good today, and my plate stays full, because I pray like it depends on Him, and I work like it depends on me.

PRINCIPLE 5—COURAGE

YOU CAN GIVE UP EVERYTHING TO HAVE ONE THING, OR YOU CAN GIVE UP ONE THING TO HAVE EVERYTHING.

When I was building my life, I felt like I had it all: my wife, my kids, my career, my home, and joys galore. Life was bliss, and the parties were plentiful. As time went on, the past life started weighing me down. All the things I had were becoming a burden that interfered with my drinking. Most of the things I had were important to me, but nothing compared to the importance of my alcohol. For some reason, it seemed to be the only thing that didn't let me down.

My wife sometimes disagreed with me, the kids didn't always obey, my job, well, that was work, my home always needed kept up, and the toys would break. But alcohol never failed me. Over time, I let go of everything in my life and held on tight to the bottle. I had given up everything and was left with one thing—alcohol.

Eventually, even alcohol quit working. I found myself stuck in the destruction of my life. Everything worthwhile was gone, and I was lost. Nothing seemed to work to pull me out. Everyone left in my life used drugs or alcohol as their survival tool, and that just wasn't working anymore. I wanted my life back, and I had no idea how to achieve that. The courts ended up with control of my life and directed me into Alcoholics Anonymous.

Through working the program that I was shown there, I was able to give up the alcohol. My life started to come back, and after some time, it all came back. I had given up on one thing, alcohol, and ended up with everything. It turns out it's true, you can give up everything to have one thing, or you can give up one thing to have everything. The choice is yours.

WHAT TRULY MATTERS IS WHY YOU DO WHAT YOU DO.

Because I'm an Alcoholic ... that's why I do what I do. That's what hit me when I heard somebody say, "What truly matters is why you do what you do." I just don't seem to think like a lot of other people. I am going to be drawn to like-minded people, and the two easiest places to find them are in bars or meetings. Those are the people I relate to. They are the people who make sense to me and the people who understand me.

When I drink, I make bad decisions. It caused nothing but destruction in my life and the lives of those around me. But there is a direct correlation between those actions and my drinking. I have no idea what may happen or what I may do once I take a drink. Without the drink, there's at least hope that I'll make sound, rational decisions. I say hope because I still don't always make the best decisions. The difference is that there's no wake of destruction at the end of the day.

People that aren't alcoholics and don't have addictive tendencies don't often understand me. I'm not weak; I'm an alcoholic. I have a physical addiction and a mental obsession with alcohol, especially if I touch it. Other alcoholics have similar feelings and difficulties, but we've found a way to overcome them. We alcoholics are a fortunate group. We know why we do the things that damage our lives, and we have a program that helps us live a life free of those things.

THE MONKEY'S OFF MY BACK, BUT THE CIRCUS IS STILL IN TOWN.

By the time I stopped drinking, my life was a wreck. Not drinking was only the beginning. By going to meetings and not drinking in between, I could feel a weight lifted off my shoulders. There was still a lot of pressure pushing down on them, but a weight had been lifted for sure. I think my head was clearing some, but only some, and I seemed to be holding steady to some degree. At least I wasn't getting pulled down any further.

When I heard somebody say, "The monkey's off my back, but the circus is still in town," I had to laugh. That was me. The weight that I felt lifted was the monkey off my back. Everything else left in my head was a circus though. I knew that this going to meetings stuff was working. With the constant pull of the monkeys gone, I was able to start working on the rest of the circus.

Life actually got kind of exciting. The more I embraced the program of Alcoholics Anonymous, the more factions of the circus dropped off. A few of the clowns try to pop back in every once in a while, but as long as I'm working the program, this neighborhood stays relatively circus free.

KEEP THE PLUG IN THE JUG.

It's pretty simple, just don't open it up. It makes me laugh because it sounds so simple, but it was impossible for me. Some of the clichés I hear are ridiculous. They mean well, but they just irritate me They almost seem condescending. They are so simple that it feels like I'm being talked down to, when in reality, I just don't get it yet.

It is a simple solution, just keep the plug in the jug, but it's not easy. Just like everything else I learn as I continue to stay sober, it works once you grasp it. Those simple, little sayings have the most profound impact on my sobriety. They make seemingly arduous tasks simple. The truth is, if I do simply keep the plug in the jug, I will stay sober. However, for me, it took a lot to do that.

It wasn't as simple as not opening a bottle. I couldn't just not open the bottle. I needed something to hold the lid on, or someone to glue the lid on the bottle so I couldn't open it. However, there was no magical pill or bottle lock, like a trigger lock, that kept me from being able to use that bottle. It took prayer, meditation, meetings, a sponsor, and a lot of work on my shortcomings. Today, I simply keep the plug in the jug and embrace everything that that entails.

INFERIORITY AND SUPERIORITY COME FROM THE SAME PLACE—FEAR.

Fear can be very confusing. Many of my actions and attitudes are directly related to fear. If I'm around people who are more qualified than me, I can be overcome with fear of not measuring up, and then I may feel inferior. I might know that I am not inferior, but the feelings can come anyway if I look at it with fear.

Since faith and fear can't occupy the same space, I need to check my feelings of inferiority and head off my fear with faith. I'm not inferior to anyone. I am exactly how God made me, and that seems OK with Him, so it should be OK with me as well. Likewise, I'm not superior to anyone. I am exactly how God made me.

Some people may have been sober for a longer or shorter time than me, some richer or poorer than me, some better or worse looking than me, and some smarter or dumber than me. None of that is relevant to my welfare. None of that is relevant to how I must feel or act. I am not inferior or superior. I am the me that God created. I can either choose to live in fear, and waffle back and forth from inferiority to superiority, or I can choose to live in faith, and grow as God leads me.

I'M NOT A BAD PERSON TRYING TO GET GOOD; I'M A SICK PERSON TRYING TO GET WELL.

For years, I couldn't seem to make a good decision. I was the bad actor in just about everything I did. Every time someone looked at the destruction of my life, I'd hear the same thing, "Maybe you're an alcoholic." Instead of accepting that I was an ass who did bad things, they wanted me to grab on to some excuse. Something like, "It's not me, it's the booze." That always seemed like a cop-out. Alcoholics Anonymous was filled with a bunch of no-good liars, cheats, and thieves who used alcoholism as an excuse for their bad behavior, but that wasn't me.

I was a guy who made decisions and knew it. I wasn't an alcoholic; I was an ass. I didn't believe in alcoholism, other than as an excuse for bad actions, but try as I may, I couldn't change. I kept trying to do good, but being bad always won. The moral dilemma was killing me. I didn't want to blame the alcohol, but I couldn't get rid of it either. Desperate, I got *The Big Book* of Alcoholics Anonymous.

After reading the doctor's opinion, I became willing to entertain the thought that I just might have a malady. I was tired of being a bad person trying to do good. With nothing to lose, I opened up to the idea that maybe I was a sick person, and I needed to get well. I surrendered my thoughts, got a sponsor, and started to work the program of Alcoholics Anonymous. THE program, not MY program.

Today, I'm a good person. I'm not perfect, but my life is no longer consumed with bad decisions. Today, I realize that I was not a bad person trying to do good. I was a sick person trying to get well, and as I stay in the fellowship of the program, I become more well every day.

GOOD JUDGMENT COMES FROM EXPERIENCE; EXPERIENCE COMES FROM BAD JUDGMENT.

Most of my good judgment came with a price. The cost was experience. All my experiences in life, if I paid attention, taught me what worked and what didn't. Unfortunately, I was much better at finding what didn't work than finding what did. Being drunk all the time just didn't afford me the ability to make good decisions. Bad judgment was my middle name. I almost never made the right decision, even when I was trying to be diligent.

I heard a lot of stories from people who were just the same at one point in their lives. They claimed that when they quit drinking, they quit having such bad judgment. In fact, I found that the experiences I heard shared day after day, meeting after meeting, largely came from the bad judgment in prior situations that taught others what didn't work in their lives.

I find a lot of people in the halls of Alcoholics Anonymous have good judgment. Like most of them, I have a vast amount of experience that came to me by way of bad decisions. It was bad judgment that gave me experiences to move forward with good judgment. All I had to do was stop drinking and let the fog clear.

GET RID OF USING FRIENDS; STAY AWAY FROM SLIPPERY PLACES, AND GO TO MEETINGS.

I've heard it said that I only need to change one thing–everything! All my friends drank and used drugs, and if they didn't, there was no point in hanging out with them. Every place I went to was slippery because if it couldn't supply me with alcohol or drugs, what was the point in going. And meetings, are you kidding me? How in the world was sitting in some stupid meeting listening to whiners talk about their downfall in life going to fulfill my desires.

I guess if I got rid of my using friends, stayed away from slippery places, and went to meetings, I would have changed everything. Those three issues pretty much made up my everything. All I knew was, I couldn't keep going on the way I was, and changing everything sounded impossible. It was simply too huge of a task to take on. Everything in my life kept pointing me to meetings of Alcoholics Anonymous, especially the judges that kept sending me to jail and treatment.

Being tired of incarceration, I surrendered and accepted the dreadful plight of sitting in meetings. Desperate to survive, I stopped going to places that served alcohol. I couldn't keep myself from drinking if it was in my presence, so I found myself spending a lot of time at home, at work, and in meetings. I didn't have to get rid of my using friends. They just seemed to disappear and wanted little to nothing to do with me if I wasn't indulging in their world of insanity.

I don't really know when it happened, or for that matter exactly how it happened, but today I have no using friends, there are no slippery places, and I seem to live in the meetings. I get to help others that tend to be like I was, watching their lives change, and making new friends daily. Alcoholics Anonymous works.

F.E.A.R.—FORGET EVERYTHING AND RUN

That's what I would do—run straight to the bottle. Every time fear came into my life, I would give up, quit, forget everything in my life, and run straight to the bottle. That's where the solution was. The problem is, when I sobered up, I found my solution had done me no good. It wasn't a solution at all, it was simply a postponement.

The alcohol would mask my feelings of failure and give me the temporary illusion that the problem was gone. Fear seemed to disappear in the presence of alcohol. My final solution was to just stay drunk, so I never had to face any of it. As it turns out, that didn't work so well. I ended up broke, homeless, and ultimately behind bars, and not the kind that serves alcohol.

I finally ended up in the halls of Alcoholics Anonymous where I learned that fear is one of the overbearing traits that created most of my issues. I was taught that if I faced those fears with faith instead of running from them, I would find that faith and fear cannot occupy the same space. By facing them with that faith, the fears were gone.

F.E.A.R.—FALSE EVIDENCE APPEARING REAL

Fear is a four-letter word. Unfortunately, it's a word we find in our lives far too often. How we look at the world and how we react to it can make a world of difference in how it influences us. Usually, our fears are unfounded. They are False Evidence Appearing Real. The stuff we worry about either isn't going on, or it's never going to happen. We worry most about the things we don't know. If we allow this stuff to run rampant in our heads, our fears grow and rob us of our joy.

When things are going along OK in our lives, we can sometimes become complacent. A challenge comes along, and fear shows up. If we're in no health, we may find ourselves Forgetting Everything's All Right.

If we get too far removed from a healthy program, we can get discouraged. Everything can start to close in on us, and the fear can become overwhelming. At that point, we are in danger of F*** Everything And Run. That attitude is dangerous. Anything we don't deal with is still going to be there when we stop running, with interest built up. Wherever we run to, we're still going to be there. We can't run from ourselves, regardless of how many times we try to.

The best thing you can do when fear comes is to meet it head on! It is possible to Face Everything And Recover. Not only is it possible, but it's how I recovered. The less things there are hanging around over my head, the less potential for fear to enter. The only way I know of to accomplish that, is to face everything that comes my way and reduce the issues.

DO YOUR BEST; LEAVE GOD THE REST.

We can't fix everything today. In fact, we can't fix everything—period. Our job is to do the best we can with the tools that we have, and to go further, we need to increase the tools we have to continue to do our best. Our best today should be better than our best yesterday, and our best tomorrow should be better than our today. It's progress, not perfection. We do our best and leave God the rest.

Our promises tell us that, "We will suddenly realize, that God is doing for us what could not do ourselves." Keep going to meetings. Keep reading the literature. Stay in the fellowship! Don't drink! Don't drug! Do your part and put in the work. In doing so, you will be doing your best. God will pick up the slack if you're doing your part, but faith without works is dead. God cannot add to your blessings if you are not prepared to receive them.

DON'T DRINK, NO MATTER WHAT.

Simple, right? Not necessarily easy, but simple. Not a lot of figuring and deciphering, just one little thing— don't drink no matter what. That seed was planted in my head when I first decided that I needed to get sober. Meeting after meeting, that seed was watered, and sobriety has grown into my life.

Throughout my sobriety, trials and tribulations have come and gone, but no matter what the difficulty has been, drinking has never been an option. I once tried to think of an option where drinking would help, like if my wife died, if some other tragic event occurred, or maybe if I was diagnosed with a life-ending disease. Then, it dawned on me, I have been diagnosed with a life-ending disease—alcoholism. As long as I don't drink, I remain in remission. If I drink, that remission proves to be temporary.

So, what's the solution? Don't drink, no matter what. When I live my life with that simple fact in the forefront of my mind, my life has value and purpose, and I am available to be of service to others. Joy abounds!

DESPERATION AND OPPORTUNITY— WHEN THEY MEET, THINGS CAN HAPPEN.

When I got to Alcoholics Anonymous, I was the very definition of desperate. Webster says that, "Desperate is a hopeless sense that a situation is so bad as to be impossible to deal with." That was definitely me.

AA was the last house on the block for me, and thus, my last opportunity. AA taught me about a Higher Power that enveloped the halls, a God that could do for me what I could not do for myself. Desperation was me, and the opportunity was AA and God. When they met, things started to happen, and the more we got to know each other, the more things happened!

It wasn't just the one-time, chance meeting like an introduction. It was actually meeting each other, spending time together, and seeing each other regularly. It was actually meeting desperation (me) and opportunity (the members of Alcoholics Anonymous and God). I had to go to meetings, get a sponsor, work the steps, and do service work. When desperation (me) and opportunity (AA and God) met, what a life that erupted!

BEHAVIOR IS TRUTH.

What I believe doesn't amount to a hill of beans if my actions don't bear out those beliefs. How I act is who I am. My behaviors are the truth of the life I am living. It's not enough for me to simply believe what's right, wrong, good, bad, or unjust. If I behave contrary to those beliefs, then the person I really am won't line up with what I believe.

The truth of my life, how I'm seen, how I'm thought of, and frankly, who I truly am lives out in how I behave. If I behave with anger and resentments, I will live an angry and resentful life. If I behave with lies and deceit, I will live a dishonest life. If I behave by judging with a critical attitude and outlook, I will live a life in judgment and fear.

However, if I behave without anger and resentments, I will live a joyful and forgiving life. If I behave with truth and honesty, I will live a life of integrity. If I behave with understanding and compassion, I will live a life of service.

I know from personal experience that the truth of my life is born out in how I behave, and my life is better when I behave right, good, and just, and when I behave with joy, forgiveness, integrity, compassion, and understanding. My life is better based on how I choose to act. Behavior is truth, so I watch how I behave.

ADDICTION IS GIVING UP EVERYTHING FOR ONE THING. RECOVERY IS GIVING UP ONE THING FOR EVERYTHING.

I was stuck in my addiction. It had taken literally everything from me. I traded everything in for alcohol. Alcohol consumed my every thought and action. It was more important than my wife, my kids, my job, my reputation, and everything I owned. I couldn't hold onto anything in my life except the bottle. I didn't recognize it at the time, but I had given up everything for one thing—alcohol. The very definition of addiction. It was all that mattered.

I desperately didn't want it that way. There had to be some way to turn that around, yet I was lost. My life could never be the same. There seemed to be no way to get any of my life back. In treatment, I was told I could recover. The concept sounded good, but it also sounded impossible. I was consumed with alcohol and didn't know how to start a life of recovery. They told me to go to meetings of Alcoholics Anonymous. There, I heard story after story of people who were just like me, or at least had been.

After they stopped drinking, they were able to get their lives back. They even got back wives, kids, jobs, homes, and everything else. I followed their path and ended up with a remarkable transformation. It turns out that addiction is giving up everything for one thing, but recovery is giving up one thing for everything.

THOUGHTS THAT KEEP ME SOBER

PRINCIPLE 6

WILLINGNESS

And not only that, but we also glory in tribulations, knowing that tribulation produces perseverance; and perseverance, character; and character, hope. Now hope does not disappoint, because the love of God has been poured out in our hearts by the Holy Spirit who was given to us. (Romans 5:3-5)

YOU DON'T HAVE TO; YOU GET TO.

I had a lot of problems that I had piled up when I finally got sober. There were so many things that I had to deal with that it felt impossible to get anywhere. Where do I start? What do I tackle first? Every time I said, "I have to do this," or "I have to do that," this guy in the meeting would say, "No, you get to."

Maybe he didn't understand. If I didn't want to go to jail, there were certain things that I had to do. If I wanted to get my license back, there were certain things I had to do. Every step forward included something that I had to do to make that progression. Every time I heard, "You don't have to, you get to," I just got irritated and felt antagonized. For quite a while, I held that as one of the stupidest things in AA.

After being sober awhile, and clearing up some of my wreckage, I started to see and think a bit more clearly. The life I had been living was heading me straight to prison or death. If not for the help, guidance, and fellowship I found in Alcoholics Anonymous, I wouldn't be here. Had I not gotten sober, I wouldn't have been able to take care of any of those issues.

The fact that I'm alive and capable of handling those seemingly impossible tasks is a miracle in itself. There was a day when it seemed like there were so many things that I had to do to clean up my life. Today, I see life through a different prism. I'm alive and capable, and now, I realize what that means. I don't have to, I get to, and I'm grateful for the opportunity.

MY MOST ADVANCED LIFE SKILL IS SHOWING UP.

Really! Just showing up to life is a major advancement for me. None of life amounts to anything if I'm not present for it. When I was drinking, I complained about life not being fair. Anybody that had to deal with my stuff would drink too. The truth is, I wasn't showing up to life.

I was so consumed with drugs, alcohol, gambling, and everything else, that I wasn't even living life. I thought I was, and I claimed I was. However, the truth is, I had stopped showing up. Drinking had made me numb to what life really was.

Now, after a little while being sober, I can see life again. I can smell it, taste it, touch it, and actually participate in it. The next day, I remember it. I no longer have to pick up pieces from the day before, when I didn't show up, because I am present for it every day. Life is awesome! Good, bad, or indifferent, showing up puts possibility to my life and enables me to move forward in it.

WILLING TO GO TO ANY LENGTH

What does that mean? Willing to go to any length sounds kind of ridiculous, or does it? Am I truly willing to go to any length? The fact is, I had better be. Nothing, and I do mean nothing, was going right in my life. Every aspect was deteriorating faster and faster. Physically, emotionally, financially, spiritually, and any other 'ally' was getting worse by the day. I had absolutely no idea how to change that, but I knew I had to, or I would die. I'd been to institutions and jail, and it seemed death was the next logical outcome. I was terrified.

When I came to Alcoholics Anonymous, I was told I could recover if I was willing to go to any length. With nothing left to fight with, I surrendered to the thought. I had no idea what that looked like, but I made that my rallying cry. I was willing to go to any length. I was three months sober when I realized what that meant. I was in the car with my wife, and I could smell the alcohol on her breath. I came face-to-face with my lack of power, and I knew immediately that I couldn't survive with that smell close by.

Any length was now clear. I knew I would drink again if confronted with that smell regularly, and I knew if I did, I would lose everything, including my marriage. I told my wife I would have to leave if I smelt it again, as our marriage wouldn't be the only thing lost if I drank. My wife and I both knew it was the truth, and her sober date is exactly three months after mine. It was that incident that made me understand the meaning of going to any length. I knew them, and I was going to make it. I knew then that I was done with alcohol.

WHEN THE STUDENT IS READY, THE TEACHER WILL APPEAR.

I never learned anything I wasn't interested in learning. Remembering back to school, the teachers that were good, all taught things I wanted to know, things I was ready to learn. The teachers that were bad, all taught things that I couldn't care less about, things I wasn't ready to learn. The teachers weren't necessarily good or bad. The student, me, was either ready or wasn't.

For years, I tried to quit drinking. The truth is, I didn't really try to quit. I thought about how much I wanted to quit but didn't actually try quitting. I went to seven inpatient treatment centers, and none of them could help me. None of them got me clean and sober.

Where was this good teacher that could help me learn how to get, and stay, sober? I went to AA meetings and never heard anything that got me clean and sober. Where was all this wisdom I was supposed to learn to help me get, and stay, sober?

The problem was that I wasn't ready to get clean and sober. I wasn't ready and willing to listen to someone else. I wasn't ready to accept the fact that I was an alcoholic, or at least not ready to take any responsibility for it or take action to do something about it.

When I finally surrendered, and was ready to do whatever it takes, the teachers appeared everywhere I turned. Some of the same people who were of no help to me before were a wealth of help, knowledge, and support. When this student was ready, there were teachers everywhere.

SOBRIETY IS A PERFECT ACTIVITY FOR ME.

One of the things I wondered about, when it came to quitting drinking, was how I was going to spend my time or have any fun. Everything I did involved drinking. There's no bowling without beer frames, and no playing softball without an ice chest in the dugout. I couldn't imagine going camping and sitting around the campfire without drinking beer and passing a joint. Without alcohol, how would I celebrate a success or mourn a disappointment? How in the world was I going to stay sober when alcohol was part of every activity that I was involved in?

I wondered about these things, but I couldn't let them be my focus. I needed to stop drinking first. My life was unmanageable, and I hadn't the slightest idea how to change that. The people in the halls of AA said they had a solution, and if I became involved with them, my life would change. I was tired of the fight, so I surrendered.

I got involved in the solutions I found through AA. I helped others in the program and did the things I was asked whenever possible. I joined the fellowship and started joining in clean and sober activities. I found that the more I was involved, the greater my joy was, and the more secure I felt. Sobriety IS a perfect activity for me!

SOME PEOPLE GO TO MEETINGS AND SOME PEOPLE JOIN AA.

For two years, I went to AA meetings that were mandated by the courts. I would get my slip signed and leave, or sometimes stay for the whole meeting. Often my wife and I would go to the bar afterwards and talk about the meeting. Getting sober wasn't part of the plan. I went to AA because I was told to, not because I wanted to. I went to meetings, but I was not about to join AA. That was just a bridge too far. How could anybody go through life, all of life, without any alcohol?

When one of my "yets," one of a severe nature, was fulfilled, something had to change. I managed to stop drinking for three months by going to two meetings a day. I went to a meeting before work and one after work. Somehow, after three months of meetings, I finally heard the saying, "Rarely have we seen a person fail who has thoroughly followed our path." There it was—thoroughly! If I was going to make it, I had to be ALL IN. No half-hearted commitments, no partial surrender, and no doing it on my own or my way.

It was time to get some hope from those who had what I wanted—sobriety! I got a sponsor, I worked the steps, took on service work, and joined AA. No longer did I simply go to meetings. I went to fellowship with my friends and grow. As a result, my life changed in almost every aspect. Life didn't become perfect, but it became more than I could have ever hoped for. I get to serve my Higher Power every day, and today, I cannot imagine a more satisfying and fulfilling life.

TRUST IN GOD, BUT DON'T EXPECT HIM TO SET YOUR ALARM CLOCK.

If I want to navigate life successfully, I need to know what time it is. I don't mean on the clock; I mean in life! In everyday affairs, I can't walk around with my head in the clouds, with no plans for the day or my life. I must set my alarm clock and get on with some actions. I trust God to guide my path. I even trust God to guide my heart. Heck, I trust God in all I do, but faith without works is dead.

If I don't take a step, God can't very well direct it, but as I continually do my part, I find that God carries the bulk of the load. As long as I'm awake and available, as long as I step out in faith, I find that my Higher Power is already up and alert and has laid out a path before me. The more I do it, the more natural it becomes.

A simple example is this: I set my alarm for 4:30 every morning. When I first started doing this, it was hard because I came right out of sleep to obnoxious noise. I kept the alarm out of reach, so it forced me to get up. I'd hit the snooze button and drag myself up nine minutes later when it went off again.

After a short time, the noise just alerted me. I could spring right up, push the off button, and get out of bed. Now, I wake before my alarm goes off, every day, but I still set it every night. I don't want to oversleep one morning and fail to enjoy what God has planned for me. I know that I can trust God to be there for me whenever I wake up, but I don't expect Him to set my alarm. Getting up and ready is my responsibility. God's got my back on the rest.

THE "RAIN OR SHINE" POLICY

When I drank and drugged, it didn't matter what the day was like. Rain or shine, I was getting loaded. It was just what I did. I called it life, cause that's how I lived. If the day was good, a nice celebration was in order. If I accomplished some goal or task I'd been working on, I deserved to treat myself, and treating myself always meant getting drunk. When I had a day off, who doesn't party. After all, there's no responsibilities on a day off.

Now, on the other hand, if the day was rough and stressful, a little alcohol would take the edge right off. If I was unable to meet a goal, I could get drunk and forget about it. Regardless of the circumstances or the day, rain or shine, I was drinking.

When I came into Alcoholics Anonymous, I was told I didn't have to drink, no matter what. Where's the solution in that? How do I celebrate success? How do I tolerate setbacks? In going to meetings, I saw hordes of people of all different walks staying sober. They talked about all the fun things they did, all the things they'd overcome, and even talked about the serenity and encouragement they felt when things went wrong.

They had figured out that drinking alcohol or using drugs did not fix any problems, it only postponed them. They had chosen a new way. Going to meetings and fellowshipping with others in the program had given them the wisdom and ability to choose sobriety, whether their life was filled with rain or shine.

THE ALCOHOLIC IS THE LAST TO KNOW AND THE FIRST TO FORGET.

For years, I was told I had a problem with alcohol and drugs. It wasn't a problem though. My bills were paid. My family was growing, and my career was soaring, so where's the problem? Whenever something would go wrong, it was the circumstance I was in, not the use of alcohol or drugs.

After all, it was the alcohol that settled me when things got overwhelming. It allowed me to refocus. Without the alcohol, how was I supposed to cope with all the pressures of life and find any relaxation? Somehow, I looked back at that thought and realized that alcohol and drugs had become my crutch, so I decided to quit.

I fought the idea that I was an alcoholic, but I couldn't stop. It was true—I was an alcoholic. Everyone in my life knew it, and I was the last to figure it out. I went to treatment and didn't drink the entire month I was there. I was overjoyed to be cured. Life looked good, so a celebration was in order. Nobody can celebrate without alcohol, so down the pipes it went. I was okay now, right?

Wrong! It only took one desire, and I had forgotten I was an alcoholic. Life immediately spiraled out of control. I almost didn't make it back to sobriety, but by joining Alcoholics Anonymous, I've been able to accept that I'm an alcoholic and understand what that means. I will never forget again.

MEETINGS—IT'S LIKE INSURANCE TO ME, AND I NEED FULL COVERAGE.

When I was new to the program of Alcoholics Anonymous, I asked the question, "How long do I have to go to meetings?" I was told I had to go till I wanted to go. At the time, I didn't know what that meant, and frankly, it didn't make much sense, but it didn't matter much either because I knew I had to. At least I knew I had to go till my probation office said I didn't anymore.

As I continued to go to meetings and maintain my sobriety, my life started to get better. I started making friends in the meetings and actually enjoyed going. In fact, some of the meetings I even looked forward to. I had found that my life was easier to navigate the more time I spent in fellowship with other alcoholics. Weird!

Go figure! I had gone to meetings till I wanted to go. You see, meetings taught me, settled me, encouraged me, validated me, and gave me purpose. Meetings helped to make sure that I stayed in the middle of the herd. Meetings protected me and insulated me. Meetings were my insurance policy for life, and I knew I needed full coverage.

KEEP IT SIMPLE STUPID!

I don't know if anything I've heard since getting sober has been more helpful than this. Nothing has played a bigger role in keeping me from going crazy. It doesn't take a lot to get me off on a tangent. The program of Alcoholics Anonymous IS simple! I'm not.

I make a big deal of little things. If things aren't complex enough, I will fiddle with them until they are. When something is too simple, there must be a flaw. So, I will dwell on it until I find a harder way. Surely more work and effort produce a better decision or outcome than something simple. I spent more time figuring and less time doing, and it drove me crazy.

I learned in the meetings that this behavior wasn't helping me. At least the experiences I heard from others bore out that it didn't help them. Once I decided to follow the advice of our program, it became simple. It's like a road map, and if you follow it properly, you get to your destination. Just follow the steps, and it really does work. Stick with the winners, go to the meetings, work the steps, and work with others. Simply follow suggestions. It's not always easy, but IT IS SIMPLE!

GOD WILL HELP YOU UP, BUT HE WON'T SET YOUR ALARM FOR YOU.

We have to be ready for God's help. We can't just lay around in a deep sleep waiting for Him to magically wake us. We need to prepare ourselves as best as we can. When I wake in the morning, I ask God to guide my steps, but the night before, I set my alarm so I will wake up. If I don't set my alarm, I'm liable to sleep in. It's quite possible that if I sleep in, I wake in a hurry, then because I'm behind schedule, I don't take the time to seek God, and off on my own I go.

Life is like that throughout the day. Certain things set off an alarm inside me that warn me of impending danger. This wasn't always the case with me. There was a time in my life when I just blazed through issues and let the chips fall where they may. The torpedoes are ready, full steam ahead. If I don't heed the alarm inside, those torpedoes hit their target, and my life explodes.

When I pay attention to life and those things around me, when I hear the alarm and wake my mind, God is there to guide my steps. He helps me up with everything I come across if I keep my alarm set. Basically, if I stay ready, prepared, and thoughtful about all I have responsibility for, I know God is there to help me when I turn to Him for assistance. God will help me up, but He won't set my alarm for me. I have to do my part.

GET OFF THE CROSS; WE NEED THE WOOD.

That statement sounds kind of harsh, but there's some reality to it. We can't just whine and snivel about our plight in life. The truth is, most of us created that ourselves. There may have been circumstances that we had no control of that started us down the path, but at some point, we fail to take responsibility for our progression in life. Poor, poor me, pour me another drink. The longer we sit on the pity pot, the deeper we fall into the self-pity that's holding us back.

Okay, so things happened. Life got hard, sad, emotional, depressing, or any other feeling you can put to it. Alcohol took you out of those feelings and made things tolerable for a minute, but once the alcohol stopped working, you were stuck. Try as you might, you couldn't drink those feelings away. Here's the question, what are you going to do about it?

You can stay on the cross, and suffer that death every day, or you can get off the cross, and get to work on your future. For years, I chose to stay on the cross. I was the perfect martyr, dying daily to show the world the terrible plight life had dealt me. The problem was, I was the one experiencing the most pain from it. It was like taking poison and expecting the other person to die. It just didn't work.

When I finally decided to get off the cross, I didn't know how. Fortunately, I found my way to an Alcoholics Anonymous meeting and was shown how. Desperate as one could be, I followed the suggestions with every ounce of strength I could muster. It wasn't always easy, but it was simple, as long as I kept it that way. I didn't get hung up on figuring it out; I simply followed the suggestions. If you're tired of the plight you're in, get off the cross. There's lots of us willing to show you how.

GOD CAN MOVE MOUNTAINS,
BUT YOU MIGHT WANT TO BRING A SHOVEL.

I love how simplistic that sounds! It's a perfect visual of, "Faith without works is dead." It doesn't do me much good to sit around feeling sorry for myself, asking God to fix it. Yes, there are times that I am so broken down, I do need Him to intervene. God will do for me what I can't do for myself, but if I don't try, if I don't do my part, then I won't know what I can't do for myself that I ask God to do for me.

We whine and snivel about our financial wreckage, asking God to help us, but we fail to look for a job. We pull our hair out because we can't handle the voices, but we seek no mental help. We complain about all the legal issues chasing us, but we don't go to court or pay our restitutions. We talk about how far our physical abilities have deteriorated, but we don't work out or exercise. We holler about God not helping us, but we don't pray or seek His guidance. The point is, we must do our part! God CAN move mountains, but you might want to bring a shovel.

FAKE IT TILL YOU MAKE IT.

You can't get to tomorrow without getting through today, and sometimes, today is not going to feel good. We in Alcoholics Anonymous are here for you. If you want what we have and are willing to go to any length to get it, live like you have it. I found that when I didn't feel like going to a meeting, I felt better if I went anyway and faked wanting to be there. I always got something if I tried.

Sometimes, I even had to fake wanting sobriety. I knew inside I wanted to be sober, but outside, I still wanted to drink. Somehow it made the moment easier, even though it always ended up with more damage, or at least as much as before. With the help of other AAs, I could even fake not wanting a drink. I could pretend I enjoyed sobriety as I saw and listened to others who had been where I was and had come through the other side.

As long as I put out the effort to try and feel like things were going to be OK and continued to live putting one foot in front of the other, continually doing the next indicated thing, things did steadily get better. Life was hard, due to all the destruction I had caused, but I could fake it through until I was well enough, secure enough, and confident enough to make it in life sober. The fellowship of Alcoholics Anonymous helped to make it all possible.

H.O.W.—HONEST, OPEN-MINDED, WILLING

You need to be three things to make it in this program with any measure of success:

FIRST, YOU NEED TO BE HONEST. Brutally honest, for your own sake. It says on our coins, "to thine own self, be true." We need to be absolutely honest to ourselves. Our self-esteem won't grow if we know we are deceitful. If you want self-esteem, do estimable things, like being HONEST. It's a must to a successful sobriety.

SECOND, YOU NEED TO BE OPEN-MINDED. If everything you know got you to this point of unmanageability with your life, then maybe you need to know something different. A closed mind will not allow anything new to enter. Listen to the things you hear with an attitude that it just might help. Just because you don't agree or haven't tried something, don't discount it. I never learned anything from someone who thought just like me. BE OPEN-MINDED. It's a must to a successful sobriety.

THIRD, YOU NEED TO BE WILLING. Our program tells us in, "How It Works," that if we are willing to go to any length, then we are ready to take certain steps. If we are not willing, we won't do the work necessary to achieve successful sobriety. It's not always easy, but it is simple. Be willing to follow suggested steps. Be willing to take a sincere look at yourself. Be willing to accept that you need to change some things in your life. BE WILLING! It's a must to a successful sobriety. This is H.O.W. we achieve successful sobriety—HONEST, OPEN-MINDED, AND WILLING.

DO SOMETHING EVERY DAY.

Take some kind of action step every single day, regardless of the circumstances. Some days, I'm working on my sobriety. Some days my sobriety is doing great, but that's no reason to rest on my laurels. There is always something to be done. Even on my resting days, those days I don't work, go out, or hang out with others, doing nothing in general is not good for me.

I've heard that an idle mind is the devil's workshop. If that is not true, I've convinced myself of it anyway. I need to be proactive in my recovery, which means I need to be proactive in my life. Yesterday's successes will not move me forward today. Well, they will, but only if I use them to move forward to the next goal or objective. Left on their own, with no further progression, yesterday's successes leave me right where I was yesterday.

Whether it's for myself or someone else, whether it's significant or seeming insignificant, I need to do something every day! There is a quote I absolutely love, "I will not allow yesterday's success to lull me into today's complacency, for this is the greatest foundation of failure."[1] I do not want to fail, so I do something every day!

IF YOU WANT SELF-ESTEEM, DO ESTIMABLE THINGS.

For years, I walked around feeling sorry for myself. My self-esteem was nonexistent. I did nothing productive for society, and certainly nothing of any lasting impact, at least not on the good side of the ledger. I couldn't seem to build myself up enough to feel worthy. I knew who I really was. I was a real piece of work, and most of my actions were less than honorable.

Something inside of me refused to believe that I was totally worthless. Although my very life showed the opposite, I just knew there had to be something worth resurrecting. Those occasional lucid thoughts pointed to some amount of worth. My problem was figuring out how to monopolize those times. How could I increase my self-esteem when I felt less than most of the time. I knew I couldn't think myself into a new way of living, instead I had to live myself into a new way of thinking, so I started to change my actions.

Rather than focusing on how I felt, I started focusing on how I acted. I started doing estimable things, and as my actions changed, so did my feelings. I found that my self-worth was directly tied to my actions. If I acted irresponsibly and lived an unmanageable life, I had low self-esteem. If I do estimable things and eliminate my selfish tendencies, my self-esteem soars, and I am a worthy example and useful vessel to be used in further service.

DITCH THAT JERK!

I'm not here to give you advice on your relationships, but I am here to give you advice on sobriety, and how to achieve and maintain it. That's called my experience, strength, and hope. In my life of drinking and drugging, I knew a lot of jerks. In fact, I was one of them, you can bank on that! When I got sober and quit being a jerk, I found it difficult to be around them, and they were really easy to spot. Self-centered, egotistical, arrogant, narcissistic, and just flat out stuck on themselves. Life is all about them. Crap! It's like I'm looking in the mirror at my old self, only I recognize it.

Anyway, I found that people in the program of Alcoholics Anonymous worked at not being jerks. They had a philosophy of helping others and getting out of themselves. I was taught that life is not about me, it's about what I can do for others. Jerks don't care about others, they don't really think about others, just like me when I was still actively drinking. If I don't stay sober, I will be that jerk, and if I hang out with jerks, I'm subject to becoming that jerk again. I will never compromise my sobriety by hanging on to a relationship that keeps a jerk in my life.

There was a time in my life when I was still drinking and that was my very definition—I was a jerk. Drinking cost me everything, and when I finally sobered up, I knew death would follow my next drink. At that point, I knew I had to be guarded in who I kept in my life. Seek sobriety first, and if necessary, ditch that jerk!

GO TO MEETINGS AND DON'T DRINK IN BETWEEN.

It might not be easy to do this, but it is that simple. If you go to meetings, and don't drink in between, you will never end up drunk. When I first quit drinking, I struggled to navigate life. I drank always, regardless of the situation. It was just part of my daily life. Avoiding alcohol and trying not to drink seemed impossible.

I noticed that, while I was in a meeting, the thoughts and desires for alcohol subsided. It was much easier, and less stressful, to be in a meeting, than to be out in the world. Since I definitely wanted to stay sober, and being in a meeting made that quite a bit easier, I went to a lot of meetings. Every time the thought of alcohol gave me the desire to drink, I would go to a meeting.

To do ninety meetings in ninety days would have required that I went to less meetings, as I was doing far more than just one a day. Pretty soon, I realized that I was going to meetings because I wanted to. I would head to meetings, even when I didn't have the desire to drink. Today, I go to meetings to enjoy the fellowship of the other members in the program, and to be there for those who may need or want something that I have. Sobriety!

CHURCH IS FOR THOSE WHO DON'T WANT TO GO TO HELL. AA IS FOR THOSE WHO HAVE ALREADY BEEN THERE.

When I think about Hell, I think about a place of absolute torment, all the time, day and night, no matter what. I don't really have a visual of what that would look like, but I feel like it would be more than something I don't like. Hell is something that never gets better, no matter what I try, or how I feel. Hell sounds like a place there's no escape from and where you just don't want to be. Sounds like my life before sobriety—a place I didn't want to be that I couldn't escape from. I was living in Hell.

No wonder people go to church. Who wants to spend eternity in Hell? Church may be a place where people go who don't want to go to Hell, but where do people go who feel like they're already living there? I tried church, and although it was uplifting, felt good, and made sense, at the end of the day, I was still a practicing alcoholic. It didn't take my desire to get loaded away. I truly believed that God could fix my life, but even in church, I couldn't find my way back to Him.

When I surrendered to AA, my life changed. As I worked the steps with my sponsor, I found my way to a Power greater than myself. I found my way back to God through a program of sobriety that was filled with others like me. People that understood the physical addiction and mental obsession I was blessed with. Church may be for those who don't want to go to Hell, but if you're tired of living there, go to AA!

DO I FEEL RESTLESS, IRRITABLE, AND DISCONTENT, OR HAPPY, JOYOUS, AND FREE?

These are really the two choices we have. We can live life restless, irritable, and discontent or we can live life happy, joyous, and free. Frankly, I grew tired of feeling restless, irritable, and discontented. I just didn't know what to do about it. Everyone I knew that seemed to be happy, joyous, and free, didn't seem to be much like me, and what worked for them, certainly didn't work for me.

As I started going to the meetings of Alcoholics Anonymous, I started seeing people that were happy, joyous, and free and seemed just like me, without the restless, irritable, and discontented feelings. Their feelings were like a barometer to the needs of their lives. If they weren't feeling happy, joyous, and free, if things weren't going the way they preferred them to, they would talk about it at the meetings. They would talk about the restlessness at the meetings. They would talk about being irritable and the discontent that they were feeling. As they talked these feelings out, they seemed to be lifted above them. Their feelings seemed to change right in front of my eyes.

If another person needed help, these same people would be the first ones to reach out and help them. They were working the program *The Big Book* of Alcoholics Anonymous suggests to us, and it had made a difference in their lives. If I want to be happy, joyous, and free, I need to recognize when I'm not, and follow the example of those that came before me and blazed a path to recovery that works.

AA—ATTITUDE ADJUSTMENT

Almost everybody knows that AA stands for Alcoholics Anonymous. Even people who have never attended a meeting, and those that aren't plagued with our malady, see those two letters and know the symbolic definition. The bumper sticker, the T-shirt, the hat, the coffee mug, and everything else with the AA symbol shouts Alcoholics Anonymous. For me, I know I'm an alcoholic, so when I see the AA symbol, it reminds me to check my attitude.

Although it may let me know that the person wearing it is in the program, or was, or knows someone who is, AA also stands for Attitude Adjustment. An adjustment is simply a small alteration. In my walk in life, my attitude needs constant attention. I can be hotheaded and judgmental if I don't pay attention to my attitude. It's usually not huge issues like it was early on in my sobriety, but left unguarded, my attitude will surely go askew, and bad things usually follow. Most of the "Tenth Steps" I have to implement are because of my attitude.

When I stay mindful of my thoughts, purposefully edit out negativity, and replace it with more realistic, positive thinking, I'm making an attitude adjustment. Done regularly, these are small alterations that achieve the desired result. It allows me to adapt to new situations even though I don't like change. Next time you see the AA symbol, take a quick look at your attitude, and make the adjustments necessary.

PRINCIPLE 7
HUMILITY

No temptation has overtaken you except such as is common to man; but God is faithful, who will not allow you to be tempted beyond what you are able, but with the temptation will also make the way of escape, that you may be able to bear it.
(1 Corinthians 10:13)

YOU HAVE ALCOHOLISM, NOT ALCOHOLWASM.

Just because I don't drink anymore doesn't mean I'm cured. I wake up every morning with untreated alcoholism because my disease is never done. I get to choose every day what I do about it. Whether that's going to a meeting, helping others, or anything else, I need to remember—I'm an alcoholic.

Alcoholism is something I have, not something I had. It's not, "I was an alcoholic," it's, "I am an alcoholic." It's alcoholism, not alcoholwasm. If I do nothing to keep my alcoholism from being active, time will take its toll, and I may partake of it again. I learned this from those who have gone before me. I must stay active in treatment for my alcoholism. It grows whether I'm working on it or not.

I need to make sure I'm growing so my alcoholism never gets too big for me to deal with. I may never be rid of my alcoholism, and it never will become alcoholwasm, but I can be free of all destruction that alcohol brings, so long as I stay vigil in my recovery program.

YOU WON'T FIND ANSWERS IN ARGUMENTS.

If I'm trying to find the answer to something, it stands to reason that I must not know the answer, otherwise I wouldn't be looking for it. I can't count the number of times I argued with someone who offered me answers.

In all fairness, some answers to some questions are ridiculous. I can disagree with them, but if I have no answer myself, then I have nothing to argue. It just points at an area of ignorance to learn. I have become aware of my flaws, and thankfully more open to their correction.

Now when I receive an answer that isn't necessarily what I wanted, I can assess it properly rather than argue points I don't know. I have found that if I seek answers from more than one source, I have a larger vision of solutions. Some issues have several levels of answers and not everybody knows them all. So, if I'm asking the questions, I obviously don't have the answer, but I know I won't find it in an argument.

MY BEST THINKING GOT ME DRINKING.

Drinking was simply what I did. I hear people say that they drank for this reason or for that reason, but I drank because I'm an alcoholic. That's what I did—I drank. Without an exception, I drank for any and every reason I could think of. That was the only solution I could think of.

If I was down, the obvious thought was to drink because that would comfort me. If I was stirred by something successful, the obvious thought was to drink in celebration. Whether I was hungry, lonely, happy, sad, tired, bored, angry, whatever, my best thinking got me drinking.

I needed to change my thinking. I needed to start thinking like the people who had success in their sobriety. Drinking, no matter what, could not be an option. That's what I was told, and that's what I would have to live by if I was to be successful in my sobriety.

As I continued to not drink, my life began to change. As I started to live a better life, my thinking began to change. I am grateful that I found Alcoholics Anonymous and its fellowship. It has changed my life!

PART OF BEING SMART
IS KNOWING WHAT I'M DUMB AT.

THIS IS BRILLIANT! I want to have an opinion about everything, but half or more of the time, I'm not very smart on the topic, so it's best to keep quiet about it. That's smart! Everyone has met someone that knows everything, or at least they think they do. They have an opinion about everything, and they sound stupid.

It's OK to not know everything. Nobody truly does, even if they think they do. The more you try to hide what you're dumb at, the less smart you seem. Being able to recognize those things that you're not smart about IS SMART!

Although the person I heard this comment from had the exact opposite opinion on almost everything as I did, it was one of the greatest sayings I've come across. Part of being smart has become learning to take what I can from others, even if we don't always agree. Those are some of the best people to learn from.

IT'S NOT SOMETHING I HAD;
IT'S SOMETHING I HAVE.

It's not that alcoholism 'was' something I had. Alcoholism 'is' something I have. It's not going away. Two of my children have diabetes, and they need insulin daily. Every day, they wake up knowing their needs. Their diabetes is not going away, but they can still live joyous, productive lives. They just have to stay aware of their disease and keep their solution, insulin, close. It's not much different with my alcoholism.

Every day, I wake up knowing my need and confronted with unresolved alcoholism. It is not going away, but I can still live a joyous, productive life. The difference is, there is no shot that I can take to balance the demons in my disease. The insulin for my disease is recovery. I need recovery daily in some form, whether that be working with someone else, going to church, seeking my Higher Power, or just hanging out in the herd. In some form or another, I need my medication daily.

I need the tools of recovery to always be close at hand, just as the diabetic needs to make sure they don't get too far from their insulin. I have alcoholism, not alcoholwasm. I am granted a reprieve daily, so long as I keep my spiritual condition embraced in recovery.

MAKE YOUR PLANS IN PENCIL AND CARRY A BIG ERASER.

Some people say that if you want to make God laugh, tell Him your plans. Others say that prior planning prevents poor performance. Which is it? Do we plan our day, or do we walk through life by faith? I think both can be true. In fact, in my life, both are absolutely true.

I don't do well when left to my own devices. I need to seek God each and every morning, before I set out for the day. If I don't, I end up in my will, and not His. I ask the Holy Spirit to guide my thoughts, then I go about my day putting one foot in front of the other, doing the next indicated thing, literally walking by faith.

However, I have responsibilities that need to be taken care of. They're not the same every day, so I make a list to make sure I don't miss something. If I don't make the list, something usually gets forgotten. Sometimes, priorities seem to change, and I need to add to the list, or even eliminate something from the day's plans altogether.

As long as I walk in God's will, and not my own, my plan is just a guideline to the day. God has absolute authority to alter those plans, and He usually does. My job is to stay flexible to what He puts in front of me and allow Him to fulfill His plan, not mine. I do my best each day to make my plans appropriate, but I make them in pencil and carry a big eraser.

I'VE NEVER LEARNED ANYTHING FROM SOMEONE WHO AGREED WITH ME.

Most of my life, I stayed away from people who didn't think like me. If their opinion was different than my opinion, I didn't need to hear it. If their truth was different than my truth, I wouldn't listen. If their perspective was different than my perspective, I couldn't see their point of view. No growth potential for me whatsoever.

When I heard this saying, something clicked in my head. After all, how could I learn something, anything, from someone who agrees with me? That would simply be information that I already know. It caused me to re-evaluate my thoughts and learning process. I could learn so much from so many if I quit being so bullheaded.

Sometimes, my thoughts, my opinions, my solutions, or my outlook are not the best. If I only seek advice from those agree with me, I'll never gain from those who may know something that I do not.

PRINCIPLE 7—HUMILITY

STAY IN YOUR HULA-HOOP.

I used to struggle with this thought: If I'm always in my Hula-Hoop, how can I grow? Don't I need to explore the horizons outside of my Hula-Hoop? I know I should stay on my side of the street as far as judgment towards others. After all, when I point my finger, three are pointing back at me. However, I wasn't sure if that was what it was talking about, or just not voicing things I don't know about.

The one thing I did know was that I didn't want to stay where I was. My Hula-Hoop was small and empty. I didn't want to stay there. I heard about a prayer in the Bible from this dude named Jabez. (It's 1 Chronicles 4:9-10 for those interested in reading this prayer themselves.) He asked for God to enlarge his territory. I never thought of it as a cry out for more property. I saw it as a desire for his circle of influence to be enlarged. As he served God, he wanted his ability to reach others to be increased.

That's how I look at my Hula-Hoop. I don't need to get out of my Hula-Hoop to grow. I need my Hula-Hoop to expand. I need to bring the tools that are outside of my Hula-Hoop into it. I need to stay in my Hula-Hoop, but I want its influence to grow.

I'M A PICKLE.
I CAN NEVER BECOME A CUCUMBER AGAIN.

Once an alcoholic, always an alcoholic. That's what they say. There's argument by some people whether we're born an alcoholic or whether we become one, but I don't really think that matters. Knowing I'm an alcoholic is what's important to me because before knowing that, I was lost. I was stuck in a pattern of behavior that made my life completely unmanageable.

It wasn't always that way. There was a time in life when I could drink, almost like a normal person. I say almost because I always felt like I wanted alcohol more than the average, and I always felt that I drank more than others. Even so, I'm still not sure if I was born an alcoholic or just became one real soon in my drinking career. Either way, an alcoholic is what I am. I can never be a non-alcoholic again.

Maybe if I had learned how to drink like a gentleman when I was younger, maybe if I had figured out self-control before life overwhelmed me, maybe if insanity hadn't felt so comfortable, maybe then I could have lived life normally. I guess I'll never know the answer to that. I've been told that I'm pickled, and I have no argument for that.

A pickle starts out as a cucumber, and the cucumber goes through a fermentation process. This process can take as little as a few days or a few weeks. Once it is a pickle, it stays a pickle. It can never be changed back. That's me—I'm a pickle. I can never be a cucumber again.

PRINCIPLE 7—HUMILITY

TAKE THE COTTON OUT OF YOUR EARS AND PUT IT IN YOUR MOUTH.

This one's hard for me. Shutting my mouth has never been easy. However, God gave me one mouth and two ears, so hearing must be twice as important. I'm good at rationalizing and justifying though. So, since I could fit both my ears in my mouth, that means my mouth is twice as big as my ears, and that kind of equalizes them.

I like to hear myself. Most of us do. But when I'm talking, I'm not listening, so even that thought doesn't make a lot of sense. When I'm talking, I'm voicing things I know. There's no room for growth or learning, because I already know the things I'm saying. If I didn't, I couldn't say them.

When I'm listening, I often find new thoughts being imparted to me. I learn things I didn't know before. My mind expands, and my life grows. Yes, sometimes it's important to let others know what we've learned that has changed our lives. That part of passing it on keeps us all moving forward. However, my growth comes from the things I hear far more than from the things I say. Besides, others need to be heard, or we won't know where help is needed for them. They will learn to listen in due time.

It's best for me to listen for two reasons. First, so I can expand my own knowledge and understanding, and second, so I can learn the needs of others, allowing me to better serve them. In order to do that, I need to take the cotton out of my ears and put it in my mouth.

IF YOU GIVE ME ENOUGH BUBBLEGUM, I'LL GET ADDICTED TO THAT, TOO.

It's not just alcohol; it's whatever I obsess over. When I smoked, it wasn't just a pack a day; it was two plus packs a day. I have a problem totally separate from alcohol, and it's me. My mental obsession with everything I like or want drags me all over the place. I never seem to be satisfied. If a little is good, then more is better.

I have come to realize that being an alcoholic is more about the problem with me than the problem with alcohol. Make no mistake, I can't touch alcohol or my life is over, one way or the other, but even without alcohol, there's still me to contend with!

Once I heard somebody in a meeting say, "If you give me enough bubblegum, I'll get addicted to that too." That made so much sense. That's me in spades. Even when it's a resentment that I know I need to let go of, I'll obsess over that too if I'm careful. Whether it's something good or something bad, my addictive traits go overboard in their reactions.

The key for me is to remember how susceptible I am to creating obsessions out of thoughts. If I stay out of my head by continuing to work an honest program, and my life is guided by the Tenth, Eleventh, and Twelfth Steps of Alcoholics Anonymous, staying clean, sober, and addiction free won't be a difficult chore. It will simply be a daily walk.

PRINCIPLE 7—HUMILITY

THINK! THINK! THINK!

I'm thinking, no, no, no! I've been in my head, and that's not a good neighborhood to be in. The more I think, the more confused I get. I don't need to, "Think! Think! Think!" I need to "Do! Do! Do!" It just didn't make sense to me.

Then one day, one of my sons was talking to me about something he had done. Some bad decision he had made could potentially cause some unwanted consequences in his life. The first thing out of my mouth was, "Son, you got to think! Think! Think!" As soon as I said it, my mind went, "OH, I GET IT!"

It's not about getting all wrapped up in your head, contemplating every decision, and driving yourself crazy. It's about looking at the pending consequences of the choices and decisions you make. Think before you act, especially if the action is questionable. Think before you speak, especially if the speech is harmful. Ask yourself, "Is whatever action I'm about to take going to help me or someone else, or is it going to cause damage? Is whatever action I'm about to take going to bring unwanted consequences?"

I've heard that when something difficult, challenging, or that incites anger comes your way, count to ten before you respond. That makes sense to me. It makes me think and gives me time to act rationally instead of irrationally.

IF I THINK I HAVE A GOOD IDEA, I RUN IT BY SOMEBODY ELSE.

My best decisions in life ended me up in a chair in Alcoholics Anonymous. That was the best I could do. It actually turned out to be the catalyst that changed my life for the better, but the destruction that got me there was due to the ideas I had about how I could live and enjoy life. My ideas never tended to be very intelligent.

Even though my decisions today are much better than before I got sober, I still find it in my best interest to run those ideas by somebody else. Life is much more productive when I get confirmation regarding my thoughts and decisions. When an idea of mine is confirmed by three others, I know almost instantly that it is in God's will.

In fact, the decision to come to Alcoholics Anonymous in the first place was not my own. I contemplated the idea, but at least three others told me it was a good idea. It was probably more like fifty people, but the point is the same. Good ideas will be confirmed by others if I take the time to seek advice. Making a decision based on my own idea, without the counsel of others, has never proven to be in my best interest. If I think I have a good idea, I run it by somebody else.

THREE PARTS— SPIRITUAL/EMOTIONAL/PHYSICAL— THEY LEAVE US IN THAT ORDER AND RETURN IN THE OPPOSITE ORDER.

When I was in treatment, my counselor told me this. I didn't think about it much when he said it. How I ended up in the shape I was in wasn't very clear to me. All I knew was simply—I was where I was. As I got sober, I could see clearly how the predicted pattern unfolded in my own life.

First, my spiritual life fell. I quit going to church, I quit praying, and I basically quit caring about anything but myself. Sometimes, it would bother me, but after a while, my emotions were numb. It wasn't so much that it didn't bother me how I affected myself or others, I just didn't feel anything anymore. I was emotionally spent and incapable of deep thoughts or feelings. Pretty soon, I wasn't sleeping right. I wasn't eating right. I wasn't getting up in the morning, and when I would get hurt or injured, I wouldn't heal very well. Physically, I was depleted.

When I was finally sick and tired of being sick and tired, I tried to lift my spirit, but I couldn't. I was drained. It wasn't until I was sleeping and eating right that I had the ability to get up, stay up, and think right. After that, I could almost feel again. The better my physical well-being got, the more I could feel my emotions, and the numbness started to fade. As my emotions returned, I was open to, and capable of, a spiritual experience. Life has been moving forward ever since.

GROWING UP

I came into Alcoholics Anonymous as an adult. As you grow up, you get a job, you get a place to live, and maybe you get married and have kids. I had done all that. I was already grown up. As I spent time in the meetings, I came to realize I had gotten older, but I hadn't necessarily 'grown up.' I had accomplished a lot of those so-called milestones, but my mind and my actions were still quite childlike.

While my life had been growing up, the maturity hadn't been. My heels were dug in when it came to my attitude and outlook on life. The more I listened, the more I understood the difference between adding years to my life and truly growing up. Lots of people came to Alcoholics Anonymous with years of life, but few seemed very grown up.

It was the ones that had been there awhile that showed maturity. The willingness to change for the better was only a start. It was a necessary beginning to my growing up, but it couldn't stop there. The ability to grow up was more than just a willingness to change for the better. It was going to take a willingness to change whatever actions came along with that.

I'm grateful to my sponsor, the program of Alcoholics Anonymous, and all the members I have met in the meetings. Through them all, I've learned that growing up is the willingness to change for the better and then a willingness to shoulder whatever decisions that requires. I'm mostly grown up today, but I continue to grow with every positive change I make in my life.

SHINING THE FLASHLIGHT INTO THE CLOSET EXPOSES YOUR SECRETS.

No matter how hard I try to hide something away, it always seems to get exposed. I stuff it away in the back of the closet where it's hidden away from everything, and I hope it never sees the light of day. Sometimes, I even forget it's there. It just sits in the closet, hidden away where they can't affect me.

The truth is, these hidden issues do affect me. They are a weight that I may not recognize, but a weight that bogs me down nonetheless. I carry that closet around with me and don't even realize it. The weight of my life is exasperating. I can't seem to fix it, because I'm carrying around a closet full of crud. If I shine light into the closet, I can see all that crud. So, the easiest thing to do is close the closet door.

The problem is that it doesn't clean up the mess; it just stores it. It keeps it tucked away, nice and neat, so it can wreak havoc on my life another day. That's not a good solution. Those hidden secrets must be exposed and eliminated, or they will always weigh me down. I no longer hide secrets away, where they can create problems later. Today, I shine the flashlight into the closet and expose my secrets, so I can get rid of them away permanently.

F.I.N.E.—
FOWLED UP, INSECURE, NEUROTIC, AND EMOTIONAL

Just fine, that's how I was. Whenever someone asked how I was, I'd say, "Fine, just fine." The reality was, I was fouled up. My life was in complete turmoil. Nothing about it was manageable anymore. The reality was, I was insecure. Everything was uncertain, and I felt assured of nothing. I was anxious and at a constant point of break. The reality was, I was neurotic, and abnormally sensitive, practically to the point of mental illness. I was obsessive about almost everything. The reality was, I was emotional. Everything revolved around my feelings. It didn't matter how things were, it mattered how I felt about them. I was easily excited and openly passionate or hot-blooded.

I'm not just fine today. Today, I'm blessed. Today, I have a Power greater than myself that isn't dependent on drugs or alcohol. Today, it seems there is a divine favor and protection over my life. It doesn't mean every day is perfect. It doesn't mean problems don't arise, and it doesn't mean I have riches beyond belief. It does mean that today, my life has pleasure and relief—which is a welcome contrast to what I previously experienced. Life is not perfect, and life is not always easy, but if anybody, anywhere, asks me how I'm doing, the answer is simple—I'm blessed!

YOU CAN GIVE UP HOPE OF
EVER HAVING A BETTER PAST.

Your past is your past. It's never going to change! No matter how hard you work, how good you are, how many people you help, how much money you make, or anything else, your past is just that—it has passed. We can't rewind life. We can start over, but our past remains the same. It will never be any better.

If we do our work in the program, we will come to a point where we do not regret the past, nor wish to shut the door on it. I struggled with that promise when I first came into the halls of AA. I had so many regrets for things I had done that all I wanted to do was forget the past and slam the door on it!

As time went on, I came to like the person I had become. All my past, combined together, made me who I am today, the good and the bad. Had any part of my past been different, the man I am today would likely be different. Also, if I forgot my past, I would be likely to repeat it, and that would be devastating. Although I can never have a better past, if I embrace who I am going forward without forgetting my past, then I can have a better present and future.

FEELING SORRY FOR MYSELF OR FEELING BETTER THAN EVERYONE ELSE?

My life was a wreck. Why wouldn't I feel sorry for myself? If you were where I was, you would feel sorry for yourself too. When I felt sorry for myself, it put the focus of the blame somewhere other than on me. I certainly didn't want to shoulder the responsibility. It was easier to wallow in my own self-pity, that way I didn't have to look at my own shortcomings.

Besides, I was better than everyone else anyway. There was no way I was going to listen to those who were beneath me. They were all admitted alcoholics, whose lives had been trashed. Weak and irresponsible people making bad decisions, that's what they were. There is one thing that both feeling sorry for myself and feeling better than everyone else accomplished— they both kept me loaded.

Both prevented me from looking at myself and my actions. Both kept me from working on the things in my life that I had control of. Both kept me from taking responsibility for my actions and the result of them. As long as I could blame someone else, or look down on someone else, I didn't have to face myself, and until I could face myself, I couldn't move forward or grow. I have learned that I can't afford to feel sorry for myself, and I can't afford to think that I am better than everyone else. The fact is—I'm not!

DON'T CONFUSE YOUR CIRCUMSTANCES FOR YOUR LIFE.

Far too often, I have heard people say that their lives suck. I would ask, "Why," and it was always the same thing. One way or another, their lives had become unmanageable, and they found themselves broke, homeless, alone, without any family, without a car, facing jail time, or any number of things that one could mention. All those things are just circumstances, and circumstances can change. Don't confuse your circumstances for your life.

If you realize that you've got a problem, if you realize that you need help, if you know there is a better way, and you're searching for a solution, then there is hope for your life. Your circumstances can be taken care of one at a time, but your life WILL get better. Your life doesn't suck; your circumstances do. I understand that it feels like your life really does suck, but it's your circumstances, not your life.

You can change your circumstances as opportunities arise. It won't happen overnight. The problems won't all be solved, and the battles won't all be won at the same time. The longer you stay sober, the more you go to meetings, the more you fellowship with others in the program, and the more thoroughly you follow the path of "How It Works," the more you'll see how your circumstances have changed.

A RESENTMENT IS LIKE WETTING YOUR PANTS; EVERYONE CAN SEE IT, BUT YOU'RE THE ONLY ONE THAT CAN FEEL IT.

OK, maybe it's not the best visual, but then again, maybe it is. When we carry resentments around, we tend to telescope those emotions. People may not know exactly what's going on in our lives, but they can sure tell the serenity is gone. If the person, place, or thing that we are harboring resentment about comes into our conversation, or worse than that, into our space, we can't hide the resentment even if we want to, but everyone else can see it. They see it in our expressions and sense it in the way we speak. Our inner raging emotion can't be hidden. However, no one else feels it. That little gift of life is reserved for us alone.

Resentments are a mixture of disappointment, disgust, and anger. They are usually elicited in the face of insult or injury. Each of those things affect us and how we feel. They usually have little to no effect on those we are disappointed, disgusted, or angry with. If we want joy, if we want peace, if we want serenity, then we must let go of our resentments. Otherwise, we might as well walk around with wet pants.

ALCOHOL IS A MASTER AND I WAS ITS SLAVE.

That's exactly how it felt at the end of my drinking. I swear I was drinking against my will. I had lost control of my faculties, and thus lost control of my actions. My life was unmanageable, and I couldn't do a thing about it. Alcohol wasn't just in control of my actions; it also had my brain. I couldn't stop thinking about the need for alcohol. I had a mental obsession that was in total control of me. Like a reed in the wind, it blew me to and fro. It was as important as food, no, more important.

I tried everything within my power to overcome the obsession, but it only got worse. Actively trying to stop felt like a slave refusing his master's order. I would feel beat up, run down, overwhelmed, and punished. Submitting to my master's orders was less painful, until it wasn't. The pain of my alcoholism got to be unbearable.

Being a slave was killing me, and I had to find a way to break free from this master to whom I was enslaved. I was too weak to break free, and besides, I didn't know the path out. I had to find a Power greater than myself to give me strength, and I needed a foolproof plan, complete with directions, to guide me out of slavery and into freedom. Through the fellowship of Alcoholics Anonymous, I found that power, and have been shown that path, and have been free from slavery ever since.

THOUGHTS THAT KEEP ME SOBER

PRINCIPLE 8

FORGIVENESS

Bearing with one another, and forgiving one another, if anyone has a complaint against another; even as Christ forgave you, so you also must do. (Colossians 3:13)

RECOVERY GIVES ME
WHAT ALCOHOL COULDN'T.

Life pretty much sucked, and alcohol made it tolerable. Facing life head-on, without the soothing comfort of oblivion that alcohol gave me, just wasn't something I wanted to face. So, I didn't. I kept myself medicated in drunkenness. That covered the pain and anguish, but the joy of life never solidified.

When I first drank, it not only covered the issues in life, but I was happy, joyous, and free. I chased that feeling for years and could never find it again. The alcohol didn't seem to work anymore. I even tried varying the way I used it, even varying the substance as well. Nothing worked. Life for me was simply going to suck forever. No purpose at all to my life, just pain and suffering for me and those I interacted with.

Somehow, I found myself in a meeting of Alcoholics Anonymous. The room was filled with people telling my story, yet they were joyful and content. I wanted what they had. I hung around and kept going to other meetings. They were all the same. Hundreds of people had found a way out of their addiction and were going through life sober and loving it. The more I hung around, the easier it was to face, without any mind or body-altering substances. I found myself in the middle of recovery; I was happy, joyous, and free. Recovery was giving me what alcohol couldn't—a life worth living.

MY SITUATIONS USED TO DEFINE ME; NOW THEY REVEAL ME.

Everything used to be a reaction. I was, in essence, the sum of whatever was going on around me. The situation I was in became the very definition of my life. I was consumed by, and consumed with, everything that happened. Life was a tornado, and who I was in it changed with every revolution. Along for the ride, blown this way and that, and never knowing who the real me was.

Whatever was going on with me defined me, and it constantly changed. I was exhausted just trying to be me, yet the real me never seemed to reveal himself. I am always amazed when I look back on my drinking and drugging days at the things that used to define me, yet never revealed who I really was.

I now realize that that's because the real me never addressed any of those situations. It was always the drunk me, the doped out me, the insecure me, the frightened me, the lonely me, the whatever me, but never the real me. It was always the altered version of me.

Since getting sober, I have learned to handle situations that used to baffle me. No longer am I a reed in the wind, blown this way and that. No longer do I allow situations to define me. Now, I take control of my actions in each situation, and I don't let the circumstances of the situation define who I am. I overcome the situation by my faith and let my actions reveal who I am.

PAIN IS INEVITABLE; SUFFERING IS OPTIONAL.

As we go through life, whether we're sober or not, pain is going to show itself. When I was drinking and drugging, the pain always brought the suffering. Sometimes, it was me who suffered, and sometimes, it was others who suffered because of my actions. No matter how I looked at it, the pain brought suffering.

Some pain, however, is good. Pain brings forth understanding and change. Growing pains are necessary for every advancement in many aspects of life. Everybody who works out will tell you that if there's no pain, there's no gain. Whenever I get injured, I feel a pain that tells me to take it easy or may even tell me to get to a doctor. When a loved one is hurt, or worse, dies, even if it's old age after a fruitful life, I feel pain. Just because there is pain in my life, it doesn't mean I have to suffer.

When my mom died, my heart hurt. Although I felt the pain of that, I was comforted that she didn't have to suffer anymore. I actually had a sense of joy, instead of a sense of suffering. When someone I'm trying to help doesn't seem to get it and goes back out, I feel a certain amount of pain, especially if it's a loved one, but I find comfort in the fact that I'm still sober.

I've found that pain is a feeling, but suffering is a state of mind. Life is going to happen, and pain is going to be inevitable, but suffering is optional, and I don't have to choose it.

GETTING COMFORTABLE IN YOUR OWN SKIN

Most of my issues, if not all of them, were of my own making. Somewhere inside, I knew this, despite the fact that I blamed everybody and everything else. I walked around acting arrogant and full of myself, but it was just a cover-up of how I really felt. Sometimes, I didn't even realize it, but truthfully, I just wasn't comfortable in my own skin.

It wasn't that everybody else knew I was a liar, a cheat, and a thief. The problem was that I knew it. On the surface I could hide it, but I didn't feel right on the inside. Since I was a liar, I didn't trust whether anybody else was telling the truth. Since I was a cheat, I didn't trust that others were fair. Since I was a thief, I better guard myself from the takers of the world.

As I worked on my sobriety, I started to realize that I was OK. There was hope for my future. I didn't have to live out the shortcomings of my life. Instead, I started to look at myself with worth. As I put value on my life, I found I wasn't so worried about others. As I lived a sober life being plugged into the benefits of the fellowship of AA, I became secure with myself.

I'm not perfect, and I've made a lot of mistakes in my life, but today, thanks to a loving God, and an awesome fellowship of others like me, I am definitely comfortable in my own skin.

ALCOHOLISM—IF YOU GET RID OF THE ALCOHOL, YOU STILL HAVE THE ISM.

I was told that the ISM stands for, "I Sponsor Myself." That's where all my trouble came from—sponsoring myself. I made all my decisions based on my wants, my needs, my desires, and my way. Why not? It was my life. After all, it was all about me, right? Wrong! I was filled up with ISM, and my life was unmanageable. I had quit drinking, but I was still sick. Getting rid of the alcohol alone just left me full of myself, and that didn't work very well.

I didn't only want to be free from the alcohol; I also wanted to be free from this ridiculously vicious lifestyle that was killing me. I was tired of making bad decisions and dragging myself down and taking others with me. The problem was that I didn't know how to get the insanity to stop.

One thing I did know was that the people in the fellowship of Alcoholics Anonymous spoke to me. I could feel their words inside: in my heart, in my mind, and in my very soul. They weren't running their lives in a selfish fashion to get through; they were helping others and being of service. They had sponsors, friends, and a Higher Power, all of whom helped them to not sponsor themselves, and to not judge what they did, or how they did it, by their own thoughts and desires. Getting out of themselves brought a new perspective and overall attitude to their lives, and that's what I desired. So, I kept coming back, kept using their advice, and kept following their suggestions. To this day, it still works.

IF YOU DON'T DEAL WITH THE WRECKAGE OF YOUR PAST, IT WILL BECOME THE WRECKAGE OF YOUR PRESENT.

All the damage I caused in my life didn't go away just because I quit drinking. I never dealt with it because I was too enthralled in my addiction. My life had been unmanageable, and I was too busy creating wreckage to clean any of it up.

After getting clean and sober, the wreckage doesn't go away on its own. If I leave it alone, it will make my new life unmanageable. However, if I address it, my life will get better and better. The tools I've received in Alcoholics Anonymous allow me to deal with it like I never could before.

My financial wreckage clears up as I stop spending money on foolish things and start paying my debt. All the damage I have caused to my relationships clears up as I make amends and stop treating people as if they don't matter. Basically, if I live my life as I outlined in my program, the wreckage of my past just seems to get dealt with in an almost automatic manner.

FOUR THINGS ALCOHOLICS SAY:
1.   **I CAN TAKE IT OR LEAVE IT.**
2.   **I CAN QUIT ANYTIME I WANT.**
3.   **I'M NOT HURTING ANYBODY.**
4.   **IF I EVER GET AS BAD AS THAT OTHER GUY...**

The problem with, "I can take it or leave it," is I always took it. I couldn't seem to leave it. Even if I went somewhere with every intent not to drink. If I was offered, I took it. Once I've had one, there is no leaving the next one, or the one after that. I am an alcoholic, and I can't take it or leave it. I only take it!

The problem with, "I can quit anytime I want," is that I couldn't. That is simply another excuse for not quitting. I was a liar, and I would tell myself anything to justify my continued drinking. I am an alcoholic, and on my own, I can't quit anytime I want.

The problem with, "I'm not hurting anybody," is that I was! For starters, I was killing myself. I was robbing time from my employer, my children, my wife, and my God. I was spending money that could have helped to take care of my family or pay my creditors. No man is an island, and what I do does affect others. If I am an alcoholic, automatically, I am hurting somebody.

The problem with, "If I ever get as bad as that other guy," is that I already am. It's just that every time I get as bad as the other guy, I lower my standards. I will always be able to find someone in worse shape than me to make me not look that bad. I am an alcoholic, and I am as bad as that other guy. When I'm in the midst of my addiction, I live in denial, and the truth is a myth to me.

GETTING RIGHTSIZED

If you were to ask me how I feel about myself, I would find a way to tell you, as humbly as an arrogant, egotistical, self-centered twit can, that I'm secure and comfortable with my life. There's a more choice, down-to-earth term I use about myself, but my editor said I probably shouldn't put it in print. I may tell you, though, that I'm honest and loyal. I might mention my work ethics or the different ways I'm of service to others. No doubt, you'll hear about my children and grandchildren. What you won't hear is my failures and my shortcomings. After all, I'm pretty big stuff in my circles, and it may not always be about me, but it usually is.

However, if you caught me on a different day, I would find a way to tell you, as pitifully as a sad, lonely, self-centered ass can, that I'm insecure and uncomfortable with my life. I may tell you I'm a liar and a user. I might mention my failures and my shortcomings or how little I do for others. What you won't hear is anything positive or uplifting. I'm a pretty big target, because everybody seems to be against me. Nothing ever goes right.

I'm somewhere right in the middle. Not everyone is against me, and I'm not all that and a bag of chips either. I don't have to be. There's always something to look up about, and I'm not the is the worst thing on God's earth. It's also not all about me. I am just what I am. Nothing more, nothing less, and that's just the size I'm supposed to be. I am something, but I'm not everything. As long as I can remember that I'm a part of, not the center of the universe, I will always be rightsized.

I HAVE A BUILT-IN FORGETTER.

My memory is good. I can retain knowledge better than most people I know. So, why do I say I have a built-in forgetter? If I read a book, watch a movie, or study for a test, I remember the storyline. I remember the plot, and I can usually ace the exam. So, why do I say I have a built-in forgetter? Do you know how many times I tried to quit drinking and drugging? Do you know how many times I looked at what alcohol was doing and swore it off? Do you know how many treatment centers I attended (and actually was sober for a month or longer while there)?

Once I gained some sobriety, I would forget how powerless I was while using. The fact that I couldn't put the alcohol down slipped right through my thoughts. I wouldn't even have to wait for my life to straighten out, just the fact that I wasn't hungover in pain was enough for me to forget about the destruction. All the pain and suffering alcohol caused to me and countless others left at the first sign of sobriety. I would always fall back on needing sanity, not sobriety.

Unfortunately, I continued to mistake a brief moment of sobriety as a manifestation of sanity. That's about as insane a thought as one could have. There's no possibility of sanity without sobriety, and it took a long time for me to realize that. I need to continue to hang around people who have my disease and still stay sober because they help me remember where I've come from. Left to myself, life is fruitless because I have a built-in forgetter.

LACK OF POWER WAS MY DILEMMA, BUT NOW IT'S MY GREATEST ASSET.

Lack of power was stopping me from being able to change my way of life. I didn't have the strength to live differently. The best I could do was maintain the daily routine I was stuck in, and even that was becoming increasingly difficult. I was constantly being drained more and more, and I couldn't seem to fight any longer. I was unable to muster up the power to turn my life around. I was being crushed by my own weakness.

Realizing that I just didn't have it in me to do anything about it, I surrendered to Alcoholics Anonymous where I had heard of people that had overcome the same dilemma. They seemed to accept their lack and draw strength from outside sources. Whether it was another alcoholic, a friend, their Higher Power, or anything else, they sat in meetings and built-up power to overcome anything and everything that came their way. It was absolutely amazing! I wanted what they had.

As I hung around for a while, I began to receive power within my lack thereof. In my weakness, I was made strong, by a Power greater than myself. Call it the meeting, the fellowship, the others who came out of their weakness, God, or whatever, I found that admitting my lack empowered me to find the help I needed in any situation. Without understanding that I couldn't do it myself, I could have never recovered. Lack of power was my dilemma, but now it's my greatest asset, as it is that which propels me forward.

F.E.A.R.—FACE EVERYTHING AND RECOVER

Really? Face everything? WOW! That's a lot! Also, quite frankly, that was impossible. I had a hard enough time facing myself, and now I'm told I should face everything if I wanted to truly recover. It was so overwhelming that I threw it out of my mind. I put it in my toolbelt, got a sponsor, and followed some suggestions. That just seemed easier than facing everything.

I continued working the steps, always giving absolute importance to the suggestions of my sponsor as I wanted the sobriety that he had. In going through literature and working the steps with my sponsor, I progressively ended up facing all kinds of things that I had buried. Stuff kept getting dug up, but because I was sober and had the fellowship that comes with joining Alcoholics Anonymous, I was able to face them, usually without even realizing that's what I was doing. It felt like I was just living life, but all the things that used to overwhelm me were now just part of it. No big deals at all! I was facing everything and recovering.

PRINCIPLE 8—FORGIVENESS

THE ONLY THING THAT REALLY MATTERS IS WHAT YOU DO.

Talk is cheap. I used to say that I was going to quit drinking and start coming home right after work. I would talk about how successful I was going to be, but talk is cheap. Without taking action, nothing happens.

People do not see the accomplishments of what I say, they see the accomplishments of what I do. Actions speak louder than words. They don't see the change in my life that I enact in my daily walk.

My life is not made up of what I think about or what I talk about. My life is made up of the things that I do or don't do, the accomplishments I achieve or don't achieve, the people I help or don't help, and the promises I keep or don't keep. The things I do are what really matters because it's only in what I do that I can help others.

That is a major part of the program in Alcoholics Anonymous. We stay sober by giving back what we received, and we don't drink! If you quit drinking and you don't work the steps, life will not be as easy or as joyful. What you do really does make the difference. If you go to meetings and help others, if you do service work and try to live life right, your life will grow.

You only get out of life what you put into it, so if you do nothing, you will receive nothing. On the other hand, if you work at life, it will work for you. What you do matters!

I STRUGGLE WITH MYSELF; EVERY ENEMY I HAVE IS INSIDE OF ME.

Outside circumstances aren't what take me down. They can frustrate me, irritate me, and cause me discomfort, but they aren't what actually takes me down. It's my inside that crushes me to the core. The pain in my head, and even in my innermost spirit, is what becomes so overwhelming that I have to silence it.

Alcohol was the perfect solution. Practically the smell alone would start to comfort me. The anticipation of what was coming after that was titillating. The silencing of pain it brought was real, until it wasn't. At some point, it made things worse.

I would wake from a drunken stupor only to realize things were no better, usually they were even worse. It wasn't the outside circumstances that really bothered me; it was the demons inside. I was my own worst enemy. In fact, I was my only enemy. Every thought and attitude that brought destruction to my life came from the inside. I had a thinking problem and couldn't change how I lived.

When I came to Alcoholics Anonymous, I learned that if I changed the way I lived, my thinking problem would follow. By following the program of Alcoholics Anonymous, with all the vigor of a drowning man trying to survive, the enemies inside seem to have given up and left. I no longer struggle with myself, at least not as much.

THERE IS A GOD, AND I'M NOT HIM.

What a relief it was to find out I wasn't responsible for everything in life. At times, it would feel like the weight of the world was on my shoulders. I wish I could say it was because I have a large, no, a huge family, or it was because I was trying to run my own business, and the many other busy things I had going on in my life. Unfortunately, the truth was that I was in charge of everything by choice.

I had put the weight on myself because nobody was good enough, and nothing else was adequate. I acted like I was God of my family, like I was God of my business, and like I was God of my finances. I played God my entire life. I can't do it all; I'm not supposed to do it all, and I don't have to try. That is what got me into this program. The result of me playing God got me a seat in Alcoholics Anonymous.

There is a God, and it is definitely not me! When I get out of the way and let my Higher Power control my life and my will, as I am taught in the steps to do, my life becomes as simple as I allow it to. Don't get me wrong, it still seems, at times, to be a daily battle, but the fight isn't such a tough one to beat. So long as I remember, it's not all about me. I'm not in charge, He is, and He will have me lead or follow wherever He sees fit as I submit myself to Him. If you don't have a Higher Power, GET ONE!

I'M A PHYSICAL BEING, LIVING IN A MATERIAL WORLD, TRYING TO PRACTICE SPIRITUAL PRINCIPLES.

It's like a bad joke. Sure, it's not always easy, but suck it up. Deal with it. Look, we all have physical needs: we have to eat, we have to sleep, etc. After all, we're human. It's a material world that satisfies those human needs, but it's our spiritual life that really controls how we end up.

Deep down, when you get to the truth of it, we are actually spiritual beings. Our inner self can communicate one-on-one with our Higher Power. Living a spiritual life should be simple for a spiritual being. We just work so hard at life ourselves that we forget that there's a Higher Power that wants to work for us and with us. We need to draw our power from Him. Our power runs out, but His is endless.

We can always draw more from our Higher Power. If you can't, maybe you need a new Higher Power. Ask Him for help in your daily life, and you will be amazed at how freely you can navigate this material world. Ask Him for help in your daily life, and you will be amazed at how refreshed your physical body feels. Ask Him for help in your daily life and enjoy the spirit inside of you as it wells up from the union with His spirit. Let your Higher Power lead you through a life you'll love.

WE DON'T SHOOT OUR WOUNDED.

I love this about Alcoholics Anonymous. If I screw up, I'm not automatically thrown to the wolves. Alcoholism sucks! It's not something that easily gets set aside. When you've got it, it doesn't want to let go of you. So many places in society throw you overboard if you have any shortcomings, and who doesn't have shortcomings.

We are all flawed in some way or another. Not one of us is perfect. Holding myself to too high of a standard was one of my flaws. I thought it protected me from failure and disapproval. After all, I had to keep my image.

That attitude was a huge part of my issue. I was afraid of being rejected if I presented myself with any flaws. As I listened to others in sobriety share their experience, strength, and hope, as I listened to them tell me what it was like for them, I realized they didn't hide from their shortcomings. They embraced their past, shared their painful experiences, and recovered from them in the process.

It showed me a vision of tolerance that I didn't find too often. Not only did it help them, but it gave me hope. When I failed, I was not alone. I could come back and honestly confess my struggles, and I was always accepted, patched up, and given some more tools. When society, or simply your own choices, gets you in a state of proverbial downhill spiral, come to Alcoholics Anonymous for help. We don't shoot our wounded.

IF I HAVEN'T DRANK TODAY, I'M BATTIN' A THOUSAND.

Every time I asked my sponsor how he was doing, he would reply, "BATTIN' A THOUSAND!" No matter what his day was like, what was going on in his life, or who was asking, he was always "BATTIN' A THOUSAND." Life will continue to go on, trials and difficulties will arise, but that doesn't mean that you're not OK! If you haven't had a drink, you're, "BATTIN' A THOUSAND."

If alcohol causes problems in your life and you haven't had a drink, you're, "BATTIN' A THOUSAND." If the things you do when you use alcohol cause your life to deteriorate and you haven't had a drink, you're, "BATTIN' A THOUSAND." No matter what goes on in your life, if you are an alcoholic and you haven't drank, you are, "BATTIN' A THOUSAND."

WE HAVE A BUILT-IN B.S. METER.

B.S. is something most alcoholics seem to be good at and seem to be full of. I knew I was a master at telling lies and making excuses. Fabrication was like a defense mechanism for me. Even if the truth wasn't problematic, a lie was more likely to come out of my mouth. It's as if I was afraid of the truth. Somebody might know who I really am if I let my reality slip out.

In fact, the term B.S. began to stand for, "Best Solution." It was always better to keep the truth to myself and tell others something contrary. That was the only way to protect myself. Let no one in and keep my life a secret. That way, nothing could be used against me.

When I came into Alcoholics Anonymous, that didn't work. I couldn't seem to get anything past the people there, since they knew all the twists and turns to my stories. Either they had heard them before or, in most cases, they had used them before. Nothing was new to them, and nothing shocked them. The funny thing was, they accepted me anyway.

They invited me back and extended their hands every time. After a while, my B.S. wasn't a, "Best Solution," it was just B.S. Pretty soon, I found myself simply telling the truth, since I didn't need to hide anything from these people. Spilling the beans of who I actually was became freeing. When a newcomer arrives at a meeting now, it's easy to tell if they're ready to get honest. It comes straight out of their mouth and is easy to decipher because we have a built-in B.S. meter.

GET A SPONSOR YOU CAN TRUST AND OBEY.

Our program of Alcoholics Anonymous has no orders given or rules demanded to be followed. On the contrary, we have only suggestions. Whether we follow them or not is up to us, but the outcome will depend on how well we follow those suggestions. The state I was in when I arrived at the halls of AA left no room for argument or decision making of my own.

My ways simply didn't work, so I proposed to follow the suggestions given to me. There was no question to that thought. It's like what happened when I was in the Marine Corps and was thrown out of an airplane. They 'suggested' that I pulled the ripcord, and the choice was mine. Whether I followed the suggestion or not was up to me. However, the outcome meant life or death depending on which choice I made.

My choices prior to coming into Alcoholics Anonymous were leading me to death. I no longer could trust my decisions and needed help in making them. After listening to others in the program, I found a person who seemed to make logical sense. I found I had a certain amount of trust in what he said and believed he had found a way out of the same affliction I was experiencing. I took him as my sponsor and followed his suggestions as if they were the instructions I was given when thrown out of the airplane.

Years later, I still follow his suggestions whenever I'm confused. I trust him, and my life has been better since I chose to obey his suggestions. My advice to others is simple. Get a sponsor you can trust and obey.

S.O.B.E.R.—
SON OF A BITCH, EVERYTHING'S REAL.

I've come to learn that we have a lot of acronyms in AA. Even right there in the title of our association, AA is for Alcoholics Anonymous. Sober as an acronym is one of my favorites. S.O.B.E.R. stands for, "Son Of a Bitch, Everything's Real" (strong words, I know, but we just talk plain).

One thing alcohol did was shield me from reality, or so I thought. The truth is, if I only postponed it long enough, reality just went on with me oblivious to it all.

Problems and troubles never went away, they just got stored until the load could no longer be carried. That weight, and all that comes with it, is what drove me to Alcoholics Anonymous. The realities of life continued to come, but slowly, they stopped scaring me as I got sober. "Son Of a Bitch, Everything's Real," became an eye-opener, almost a rallying cry of success.

As I faced each situation, and worked at doing something about it, the problems and troubles started falling off instead of piling up. Bit by bit, piece by piece, the weight was being reduced. The load was no longer unbearable. By embracing the fact that everything IS real and facing those realities with a clear and sober life, my perspective has changed. It has grown.

"Son Of a Bitch, Everything's Real," is no longer an exclamation of surprise and fear. It is now a simple statement of fact, reminding me that if I don't deal with it, whatever it is, it will present itself anyway, and the weight will become overbearing.

EXPERIENCE, STRENGTH, AND HOPE

We're called to share our experience, strength, and hope. That's all we can do. I can't share anybody else's experience, strength, and hope, because my life is not theirs. I haven't had their experiences. In fact, the more I'm around the halls of Alcoholics Anonymous, the more I see how similar our experiences are in so many aspects, but you get what I mean.

My experience comes from all the things that have destroyed me in my intoxication and all the things that have helped me in my sobriety. All the things that have worked, and some of the things that didn't work, showed me that I can be successful with sobriety. I can share that experience with others. Most of my experience came from listening to the experiences of others and what helped them.

My strength comes from the guidance I get from my Higher Power and my fellowship with others in the program. The more time I spend with others in the fellowship, the stronger I become. The more aware I am of God's guidance, the wiser I become in that strength.

My hope comes from the successes I see on a regular basis. Not just from everyone around and those I hear share, but from the successes in my own life that are even more overwhelming. The promises really do come to pass, sometimes quickly, sometimes slowly, but they do come.

PRINCIPLE 9

FREEDOM

Heal me, O Lord, and I shall be healed; save me, and I shall be saved, for You are my praise. (Jeremiah 17:14)

LET IT HAPPEN.

We have a saying posted in most of our AA halls that says, "Let go and let God." I was so busy being in charge that letting God handle anything wasn't even a thought. I would spend most of my time in my own head, figuring out how to make things happen. Most of the time, it was a dismal failure. I was constantly trying to force the results to match what I wanted.

It was exhausting. I rarely had the semblance of success. When I spend my time and energy concentrating on my sobriety, and worry less about the other issues, those other issues seem to dissipate. I have found that forcing things to happen when I'm loaded, in both cases, is harder work than it needs to be.

My ability to change behavior and straighten out my life are not always things that I have to work hard at. Sometimes, I just need to put one foot in front of another and do the next indicated thing. I don't always have to force the outcome. Sometimes, I just need to let it happen.

IF YOU DON'T DRINK, YOU WON'T GET DRUNK.

It sounds logical to me, but is it really that simple? It's a true statement—if you don't drink, you won't get drunk. But how do you not drink? That's like not breathing. It just seems automatic and comes naturally. I never set out to drink; I just drank. I either didn't need a reason or everything was a reason. I don't know which, but drinking was as normal as breathing.

If I was happy, I drank in celebration. If I was sad, I drank to drown my sorrows. If I was scared, I drank my instant courage. No matter the situation, I drank! Then some smart-ass says, "If you don't drink, you won't get drunk," and I just wanted to hit him in the face. Man, do I wish it was that simple.

The truth is, it is that simple, but it's not always easy. Life is going to happen, and sometimes, it's not going to be comfortable, but I don't have to drink over it. I have a fellowship of people, and friends who have become family, that help to guide me and shoulder my difficulties.

I have heard it said that a problem shared is a problem halved. In my life, I am surrounded daily by a group that depends on one another. My problems are halved, and halved again, as we stand together against our common issues. We know that if we don't drink, we won't get drunk, and we need each other to accomplish that.

LET GO OR GET DRAGGED.

This saying hits me on two fronts. One, I can let go of my addiction or get dragged into the depths of Hell. The other, I can let go of my stubborn attitude or get dragged into submission to all the pains that come with prolonged use. Both require that I let go. Both suggest that the drinking and drugging need to stop. Both point out that I will be dragged if I don't stop.

The bottom line is that life is going to continue to keep getting the same thing. Even if my mind is guiding me into better truths, if I don't let go of my past actions, I will be dragged along the way, regardless of my mind. I need action, not just thought, and the action I need must be different than the action of my past.

This reminds me of that saying, "You can't think yourself into a new way of living, you need to live yourself into a new way of thinking." If I do not let go, nothing will change. I need to let go of my addiction, let go of my bad attitude, let go of my stubbornness, and let go of my will, so that I can embrace His will for me. I need to let go of my ways, one way or another, or I will be dragged.

LEANING IN, LEANING ON, LEANING BACK

Getting sober turned out to be something I couldn't do on my own. I tried as hard as anyone could, but it was futile. The truth is, I didn't really put full effort into getting sober, because I couldn't. I didn't know how.

When I came into Alcoholics Anonymous, I was told there was a path to follow, and if I followed it thoroughly, there was little chance of failure. Leaning into the program, giving it my all, was the start I was told to make. As I continued on that path, I found that I needed others in the program. Relying on my own mind and actions was not enough.

It was the ones who had gone before me, who had made it down that path, that inspired me. Following them was my only real hope. Leaning on their experience and guidance, using their compass of life, made it possible for me to stay on that path. Without them, I wouldn't even know what that path was.

Following them down that path has allowed me to lean back and see the whole vision of sobriety. It's become a vision worth looking at, and it's become a vision I can now share with others.

I started to understand my life as I started leaning into the program of Alcoholics Anonymous. It started to improve as I started leaning on the others there, and I became of service to those still hurting as I began leaning back on all I had learned.

IT'S A RECIPE.

I absolutely love this. There is not one, single thing that keeps me sober. When I'm feeling spiritual, I may like to think that it's God, my Higher Power, and His grace that makes it possible. However, the truth is, not even God will keep me sober against my will.

God is definitely a major ingredient in the recipe, but there's a whole lot more that goes into the making and maintaining of my sobriety. I could not have gotten sober without the meetings and all that I learned from them. I couldn't stay sober without the continued knowledge and understanding that I received from going to meetings.

Working the steps was a major part of getting sober and living them helps to keep me sober. I don't believe I could gain the joy my Higher Power has in store for me without them. My sponsor helped guide me in understanding what sobriety really is, and regular contact with him helps to ensure that I'm staying on the right path to keep it.

Service work and meetings kept me involved in the program as I was getting some sober time under my belt, and it keeps me involved today. There's other factors, like having a sponsee to be accountable for, helping the newcomer, fellowship with others in the program, sharing when asked, and listening when needed. The longer I stay involved, the more I find little ingredients here and there to add to the recipe, which keeps making the flavor of my life taste better and better.

I'M NOT WHAT I SHOULD BE, AND I'M NOT WHAT I WILL BE, BUT I THANK GOD, I'M NOT WHAT I USED TO BE.

It's progress, not perfection. So long as we strive for perfection, we will always show progress. I know I have not, quote-unquote, "arrived." I am not what I should be in more ways than one. I have not overcome all my shortcomings. Sometimes, it hurts when I look at the man in the mirror, but I'm encouraged when he looks back and says, "You got this! You're not what you will be yet, but it took some time to become the hot mess that started out this journey."

I am glad that I have a good relationship with myself now. I can process things, instead of reacting to them. My solution to everything in life is no longer alcohol. I thank God for guiding me to Alcoholics Anonymous because it's the program, and the people of that, who have helped me not to be what I used to be.

I am no longer an unreliable spouse, father, and employee. I am no longer a person people avoid. I no longer have to hide from the bill collector. I no longer have to avoid phone calls. I know where I am when I wake up in the morning, and I feel good. I may not be what I should be, but I also know that I'm not yet what I will be. If I continue to do this one day at a time, I will never again have to be what I used to be.

LIVE AND LET LIVE.

When I first read this hanging in one of the AA halls, it didn't make much sense to me. It kind of reminded me of the times of peace, love, and dope in the 60s. Do what you want, and let others do what they want. Just live and let live. If it feels good, just do it, and don't worry about what others do. After all, they should be able to do whatever feels good to them, too.

I had it all wrong though. After being around for a while, like everything else, live and let live made sense, but not in an improper way, as I had previously thought. It's quite simple. I have no control over people, places, or things. Not really. I can impose my opinions, my attitude, and my will from time to time, but it only has whatever effect others allow it to have.

Others will live as they choose, but I don't have to allow that to affect me. I need to live my life, not someone else's. I need to keep my side of the street clean, and not worry about everybody else's side of the street. I need to live my life right. If I believe someone else isn't, I do not have to hang out with or associate myself with them. My job in life is not to change them! Sometimes, I need to get over myself, and simply, live and let live.

THROW THE THOUGHT OUT OF YOUR HEAD.

I've heard it said to, "Think the drink through." I understand that idea and believe it to be good advice, but it didn't work for me. Every time I tried to think the drink through, I seemed to get stuck at the good feeling of it. I couldn't seem to go all the way through to the pain, and then I fantasized about the pleasures of it.

My sponsor told me, "Throw the thought out of your head." This was what I needed. If a thought of a drink comes into my head, I throw the thought out. I simply occupy my mind with something else. I can pick up a book or watch a show. I can help another who is suffering or go to a meeting. Anything that takes up my thoughts to keep my mind off using alcohol or other substances will work.

It not only works with alcohol, but with every improper thought that comes into my head. No matter what the circumstance, or situation that it brings something negative into my head, especially if it's the thought of a drink, I simply, "Throw the thought out of my head."

MEETING MAKERS MAKE IT.

I like to hang out and socialize with like-minded people. I seem to be naturally drawn to them. So, it's no wonder I liked partying and going to bars; that's where my people were. The thought of getting sober was terrifying. Life without my kind of people sounded lonely. The normal people just didn't think like me and were confusing to my soul.

Due to very specific orders from the court and treatment, I was directed to Alcoholics Anonymous. It wasn't long before I realized that these were the same kinds of people that I hung out with at the bars and parties. The faces were different, but when they spoke, I could feel it inside that I could relate. These were my people, but most of them were happy, content, productive, and even successful.

I would sit and listen to their stories, and I could relate to almost all of them. Not only was I able to fellowship with like-minded people in the meetings, but I was able to understand and comprehend the conversations, and I was able to grow. The more I went to meetings, the more I grew.

My life started changing. The more I went to meetings, the more comfortable I felt in my own skin. My difficulties got easier. Problems cleared away from my life—not all of them, but consistently, more of them cleared away with each meeting I attended.

Every time someone would go back into their previous lifestyle, there was one overwhelming theme to lead up to it—they had quit going to meetings. I can't afford to ever drink again! It would surely kill me. My defense is to stay involved and regularly make it to meetings, because meeting makers make it.

I GET TO.

There seemed to be so many things I had to do when I first got sober that I was exhausted just thinking about them. I had to go to management. I had to go to court. I had to go to probation. I had to go to meet with my community corrections office. I had to pay fines, I had to attend meetings of Alcoholics Anonymous, and the list went on. Every time I'd say, "I have to do this," or "I have to do that," this guy in AA would say, "No, you don't have to, you get to."

Hearing him say that probably pissed me off more than anything else in my sobriety. I didn't get to go to court, I had to, or I'd end up in jail. It truly irritated me that this guy who had already done all the stuff he had to do when he first got sober, made it seem like I was lucky to go to court. I was lucky to get to go to anger management, and lucky to get to deal with all that other stuff. Even my wife caught on to his comments, and she stared saying it.

After a while, I got used to hearing it, and it started to sink in. I could be in jail, an insane asylum, or worse yet, dead. Instead, I get to live life. Even with all its difficulties and responsibilities, living life with the op-portunity to do all those things was far better than the alternative. Some people never get the opportunity to do all those things. Having the ability and freedom to fulfill the requirements put on me is actually a blessing. Today, I don't have to do anything, I get to.

THE MORE I CHANGE MYSELF,
THE MORE OTHERS AROUND ME CHANGE.

I've always judged others. Looking at someone and seeing their faults has always been easier than seeing my own. I am usually not in front of a mirror, so it makes sense to me. Others are what I see. There were a lot of things in my life that needed to change, but I didn't notice them.

I was looking at the changes everybody else needed to make. If only they would change, things on my end would be much better. It took me a long time in life before I could see my own faults. I had buried them and hidden from them for so long that they were difficult to notice, at least for me. It seemed that everyone else could spot them quite easily.

When I quit drinking, I suddenly started noticing my shortcomings. Without the fog of substance abuse, it was like I was always looking in the mirror. I quit noticing the faults of others, because my own were always in my face. Without drinking, I was able to work on those shortcomings and begin to change them, one after another. As I did, I realized that it was my own faults, not the faults of others, that had been the problem all along.

All of a sudden, the judgment I had been passing on others started to disappear. I saw them with a different lens, and most of their faults didn't even exist. I had been projecting my lack and my issues onto them. I've now found that the more I change myself, the more others around me change. In reality, the only change that really came about for them was how I looked at them, and that came when I learned how to look at myself.

THERE ARE TWO DAYS I HAVE A PROBLEM WITH: YESTERDAY AND TOMORROW.

Life is tough enough without trying to live it somewhere other than in the here and now. There is enough going on right now to take up all the time I have. Yesterday is gone. I can't get it back. No matter what went on, good or bad, all I can do is learn from it. I can't change it. It already happened; it's the past. When I dwell on things gone, I accomplish nothing in the moment I'm living in.

I've got issues that crop up if I don't stay focused. My energy needs to be focused on events, issues, and ordeals of the present. I need my focus on today. Tomorrow isn't here yet. In fact, it may never come. In the event that it does, which it most likely will, I have no idea what it's going to bring. Whatever it does bring is irrelevant if I don't make it through today. There's only so much planning I can do for a day that hasn't come yet in which I don't know what it's bringing.

Besides that, my history has taught me that if I don't spend today taking care of today, I'll end up in tomorrow with yesterday's agenda still to take care of. That doesn't make for a very productive "today" when it gets here. The best thing for me is to stay focused on completing the things of today, then I'll find I'm automatically overcoming the things of yesterday and preparing for the things of tomorrow.

THERE IS A SOLUTION.

It tells us this is in *The Big Book* of Alcoholics Anonymous. It's the title of our second chapter, and I encourage you to read it. It's good news. Thank God, "There is a solution!" Imagine where we would all be if there wasn't. I know I'd be in prison, institutionalized, or even dead. No doubt about it.

When I walked into my very first AA meeting, after deciding I couldn't live my life in active addiction anymore, I was so relieved someone was there. That was the beginning of my solution. How sad it would have been if I showed up for help and no one had been there. We are all part of the solution. We need to pass on to the alcoholic that still suffers all that we have learned.

There are many pieces that make up the solution for alcoholism, and between the group of us, the pieces fit together. Like a puzzle, if you don't have all the pieces, you may be able to see what the finished image shows, but it's much clearer and complete if you have all the pieces. Find the pieces to the solution! You can find them by listening to the stories of others, reading the literature, and working the steps!

IF I'M NOT DONE,
NOTHING YOU SAY CAN KEEP ME HERE.
IF I AM DONE,
NOTHING YOU SAY CAN DRIVE ME AWAY.

I came in and out of the halls of Alcoholics Anonymous for quite a while. I heard what people said. I even understood and agreed with most of it, but I would leave the meeting and go get drunk anyway. Sometimes, I would go straight to the bar from the meeting. You see, I wasn't done. I wanted to be, but I couldn't seem to carry that thought beyond the meeting.

If I wasn't surrounded by sober people, I didn't think about sobriety. I only thought about silencing that craving that was uncontrollable. Nothing anyone said could overpower the control alcohol had on me. I felt doomed. My fight was practically gone. Life seemed futile. I could produce no useful results. I knew that if I kept on this path, I would surely die, possibly by my own hands.

At some point, I had to surrender. Being at the end of my sanity, I did just that. My fight was gone, and I gave up fighting. I didn't know how I was going to move forward, but by joining the fellowship of Alcoholics Anonymous, I was shown how. As long as I stayed in the program, I gained strength and even some tidbits of wisdom.

After a while, I had a little stability in my sobriety, and I knew I didn't ever want to lose it. I had been shown a better life, and I liked it. I never wanted to go back to the way it was when I was drinking, so I didn't, I haven't, and I won't. AA taught me how to live sober, and nothing anybody could say will ever drive me away.

I CAN'T CONTROL THE WIND, BUT I CAN ADJUST MY SAIL.

Life happens. No matter what I do, shy of killing myself, life continues. The wind of life blows stuff against me, sometimes knocking me back or completely over, but I can adjust the sail of the ship that is me and my life stabilizes. If the problem is the wind, I'm screwed! I have no control over the wind, because it blows however Mother Nature sees fit.

I can let it blow me over. I can let it blow me down its own path. I can lean against it and struggle to stay upright, going nowhere as I fight against it, or I can do something different. I can adjust my sail, and let the wind of life blow me down the path God intended for me as I submit to the simple program of Alcoholics Anonymous, and let my Higher Power guide me.

TREATMENT IS DISCOVERY; AA IS RECOVERY.

If you want to learn about alcoholism to discover if you're an alcoholic, go to treatment. If you know you're an alcoholic and you want to recover, go to AA. It's really that simple for me. I never could embrace Alcoholics Anonymous because I didn't believe it was a disease. If I could just get sober, I would think right, and then I would quit screwing up my life.

After seven in-patient treatment centers, I finally retained knowledge about the disease of alcoholism, and yes, I discovered that I was an alcoholic. This was actually quite empowering. Heck, it's our First Step. Once I knew I was an alcoholic, the things I had heard in those seven treatment centers started to make sense.

All of them told me to go to Alcoholics Anonymous. All of them told me to attend meetings regularly. All of them told me to get a sponsor. All of them told me to work the steps, yet all I had was knowledge. I had discovered that I was an alcoholic, but I hadn't recovered. Every time I got out of a treatment center, I just ended up blasted again.

Finally, I surrendered to the idea that Alcoholics Anonymous might be my last hope, and that the active members possibly could show me the way to sobriety. I wasn't filled with hope, but most people in meetings were. I wanted what they had. I got a sponsor. I followed his suggestions, and I worked the steps. I started helping others and serving in Alcoholics Anonymous, and guess what, I got sober and stayed sober. Treatment is discovery, but AA is recovery.

HOW'S YOUR NOW?

When I look back on my past, it can be depressing. I know our promises say I will not regret the past, but truthfully, there's a lot of my past I wish I hadn't done. Yes, I learned from it, and I'm able to help others because of it, but my life before sobriety caused pain to myself and countless others. That can never be erased, but I don't have to live there.

In thinking about tomorrow, my brain can tend to get overwhelmed. There's so much to take care of and so little time to do it. Do I even have the ability, let alone the desire? Looking ahead at all of it makes me want to give up. Sometimes, it's just too much. The fact is yesterday's gone and tomorrow isn't here yet. All we truly have is today.

Today is what matters, and frankly, today usually has plenty to deal with on its own. That works out perfectly for me though. I've been blessed with a program that teaches me to live one day at a time. As I pay attention to today, yesterday's issues shrink, and I don't have to worry about what might happen tomorrow. It's the now that I can manage today. So, how's your now?

I AM TIRED OF PAYING SUCH A HIGH PRICE FOR SUCH A LOW STANDARD OF LIVING.

Boy is that the truth! I can't even add up all the money I have spent regarding my addictions. The cost of the alcohol and drugs that I personally used was a big enough expense. The rest of the costs were astronomical.

There was the gas used to get to the store to buy alcohol, or to get to the drug dealer's house to get my next fix. There were the rounds I bought for other people, friends of mine, or even people I'd never seen before, and most likely never would again. There were the foods I ate while food tripping with munchies, and the foods I wasted while food tripping. The money that disappeared due to my grandiosity. Even the compassion and generosity that I legitimately had for others was lost in that grandiosity.

It added up in larger and larger ways as the troubles came: the lawyers for the DUIs, and the raised insurance rates, fines and court costs, not to mention the treatment costs, and lawyers for drug charges and assault charges. The cost of constant vehicle repairs from the crashes, usually my vehicle and someone else's was awful. Somehow, as huge as the number was, those costs were paid. I had to cover those costs in order to use it again. For all that money, I had nothing but as low a standard of living as I could imagine.

My life, outside of financial decay, was morally, ethically, emotionally, and spiritually bankrupt. I was beyond tired of paying such a high price for such a low standard of living. I joined Alcoholics Anonymous and was amazed with what I found. I found a fellowship of men and women who had paid a high price too, but they had solved their problem. They had what I wanted, and today, I have it, too. It's a life that costs far less than its value, and I can't seem to give it all away. I just keep filling back up.

THINK THE DRINK THROUGH.

We must remember how dangerous alcohol is to us if we drink. We must remember what drinking brought to our lives and the destruction during and after. We must remember the hangovers and jail time, as well as the pain we caused others and ourselves. If the comfort of a drink seems like a good idea, "Think the drink through."

What comes after you take that drink? Do you make it home? Do you make it to that meeting? Do you end up in the back of a police car, in the hospital, or even in a coffin? Does your life get better? If we think the drink through to the end, we must admit that taking the drink in the first place is insanity.

If we remember all the wreckage that comes because of our drinking, then it can empower us to leave the drink alone. Think the drink through before you take it, and then make an informed decision on whether or not you want it. If you're serious about saying sober, go to a meeting, or call a friend that's in the program, but don't succumb to the thought of a drink. Think it through!

HOW FREE DO YOU WANT TO BE?

Totally! I mean, why not? How does this sound, "I'm partially free," or "I'm almost free." Neither of those work. Our Creator gave us free will, and that freedom is part of our very make-up. It's embedded into our DNA. That is most likely the biggest reason for my drinking. I felt like it made me completely free. I could let loose and be myself because all my inhibitions were gone. I was as free as I wanted to be, or so I thought.

When my drinking started to cause problems in my life, I became a slave to the debtors and creditors I was neglecting. I tried to quit and found that I had become a slave to the very thing that gave me my freedom. What was I going to do? The spiral down ended with a thud as I hit the bottom.

As a marine, the thought of surrender is foreign. You get free by winning the fight, not by surrendering. Yet I was told that I needed to surrender to win. What kind of fools had I hooked up with? However, they seemed free, truly free, and the ones that had been around the longest seemed to be the freest. I wanted what they had, so I surrendered to the idea of following the suggestions of those who had what I wanted.

The closer I follow those suggestions, the freer I feel. So, it has become really simple. I surrender to my Higher Power every morning, put one foot in front of the other, and do the next indicated thing. Life is simple for me, and I am as free as I want to be. Totally!

STAY CLOSE TO GOD; PUT ONE FOOT IN FRONT OF THE OTHER AND DO THE NEXT INDICATED THING.

That is my life in a nutshell. I wish I would have lived this way for my entire life, but drugs and alcohol kept me working hard. Trying to hide how I was living was a chore. Trying to pray, when I felt I wasn't worthy of God's hand on my life, was painful. The reality is, if God's hand hadn't been on my life, I wouldn't be here. I'm grateful that He walked with me, even when I wasn't walking with Him.

It took some time in sobriety for me to realize how to keep it simple. I always wanted to work hard at staying sober. I struggled to put off my vices and bad habits. Staying close to God was difficult because I didn't feel worthy of being in His presence, and frankly, I was usually hiding from Him.

As time went on, as the cobwebs cleared, and as I worked the steps of Alcoholics Anonymous with a sponsor, I came to see the simplicity of the program in my life. Yes, there's work to do in staying sober, but most of it is work I'm not capable of doing on my own. With everything there is to do in life, how does a guy, afraid of being in his own mind, figure out what comes first or what comes next? It's like having a new job and not being sure which responsibility that you were given is the next step in the process.

That's where your boss, or mentor at the company, comes into play. They give you guidance and instruction. I need the same help in my new life of sobriety. Today, I get up each morning, and I ask God to guide me. I stay close to Him all day; then, I put one foot in front of the other and do the next indicated thing. Life turns out pretty good if I keep it that simple.

WE EACH HAVE TWENTY-FOUR HOURS.

Yesterday's gone, and tomorrow isn't here yet. All we have for sure is today, these twenty-four hours we're in the middle of, and we should be thankful for that. Twenty-four hours is hard enough to handle. God help us if we had to think of more than that.

We really can only do today. Whatever went on yesterday, whatever mistakes and screwups, whatever successes and accomplishments, they are in the past. We can't rest on our laurels and be stagnant today. Each day, we are given a fresh twenty-four hours, and that's our responsibility for the day.

Yesterday's successes die if I do not promote their progress forward today, and tomorrow's accomplishments won't come to pass if today's planning isn't complete.

You see, these twenty-four hours are enough responsibility for us, and handling them appropriately allows the past to be properly put to rest and the future to be properly prepared for. All of this happens simply by living these twenty-four hours to their fullest. Dwelling on the past or tripping on the future does us no good. We are part of unbelievable, life-changing events happening all around us when we are successful in the twenty-four hours we each have.

FISHING FOR SOBRIETY

Ponder that title carefully. I think that's what I was doing for a long time. I just didn't know where the good fishing holes were. Me and my fishing pole (my attitude) wandered through life, fishing everywhere I could think of, but never catching anything but trouble.

I went to church and got prayed for, with and without hands laid on me. I was anointed with oil, and I went to treatment, both inpatient and outpatient, seven times. I swear I prayed to God for deliverance, but I don't know if I even knew how to pray, or who I was praying to. What did sobriety look like anyway? It had to be better than the life I had. I just had to find the right fishing hole.

Through a series of events, I found myself in Alcoholics Anonymous. The people that spoke seem to have caught the elusive fish called sobriety. They didn't even have to travel far. No matter where they were in the world, they knew how to find the perfect fishing hole. You catch sobriety in the meetings. They are the perfect fishing holes, so go to a meeting. That's where you're going to be able to fill your boat if you're fishing for sobriety.

WE TREAT OUR DISEASE WITH ABSTINENCE, BUT THE SOLUTION IS IN THE STEPS.

If all you do is stop drinking, your life will most likely get better from that alone, but abstinence is not the solution. It's how we treat our disease that makes us capable of finding the solution. That solution is in The Twelve Steps of Alcoholics Anonymous. These steps are the foundation for a life of joy.

I know many people in the program who have not worked the steps, and it shows in some of their lives. They aren't really plugged into the full power of the program. They lack a joy they don't even know exists. The easier, softer way is spelled out in "How It Works." The steps simplify a breakdown of how it works.

Abstinence keeps me sober, but the steps straighten out my life. Each and every one of them fulfill a need to set my direction, and each and every one of them help in the process of fixing my life. I started righting the wrongs, mending relationships, and fixing my finances.

The promises really do materialize. First, the steps taught me to surrender, which took the control problem away. Then, the steps taught me to set things right, which brought forgiveness and enabled me to move forward. Finally, the steps taught me to live life abundantly with integrity and service, which created a life of joy.

SOBRIETY IN PROGRESS

I'm so glad to know that I don't have to worry about being perfect, cause that just ain't gonna happen, no matter how hard I try. I do need to try though. I'm not going to move forward in life if I don't set my eyes on things ahead. Once my eyes are focused forward, I need to put actions in motion. I call this—sobriety in progress.

Getting sober didn't mean just stopping drinking for me. Oh, it was a big part of it, as nothing could have come after that if I hadn't gotten sober first, but to quit ingesting alcohol into my system was only the start. It was a necessary start though, that's for sure.

As my vision of reality cleared and rational thought returned, I could see the possibilities of a future. Beyond today's satisfaction had never crossed my mind before. I saw something that people called life, and it looked desirable.

As I continued to walk alongside the fellowship of Alcoholics Anonymous, I learned that getting sober isn't an event, it's a lifestyle. At the end of my life, I want to present myself to my Higher Power with a clean conscience. Life's challenges didn't end when I quit drinking and neither did my disease. I stay connected so my life continues to move in the right direction, ensuring I live a life of sobriety in progress.

DRINKING IS BAD FOR ME. AA IS GOOD FOR ME. EVERYTHING ELSE IS NEGOTIABLE.

So many simple, common-sense sayings like this used to escape me, but if I keep it simple, then it really is believable. Drinking is bad for me, and I should never do it. AA is good for me, and I should do it often. Everything else, I can look at and decide whether it's good or bad for my life.

What I can't figure out is why I seemed to make it so difficult. Simple was always too simple. I needed to figure out what to do in every situation. I really don't know why. It could be that I didn't trust anyone or anything but myself, or it could be that I had to be the final say in everything. How could I trust anyone, or anything else, when I was such a liar, cheat, and thief? I certainly wasn't going to do anything that wasn't my idea. In my mind, I was the best one to decide my destiny, despite the fact that my life was unmanageable. I need to keep it just as simple as the statement: "Drinking is bad for me; AA is good for me. Everything else is negotiable."

Yes, drinking is bad for me; so, no matter what, I can't drink. It never has to be given any consideration again. Drinking is NEVER an option, period. AA is good for me, so, no matter what I face, I need to stay in the program. I need to hear the stories of others in meetings, and I need to share my experience, strength, and hope as well, not just for my own sobriety, but also, because I am responsible to others who need help. This is the only way I'll be prepared for, and capable of, negotiating any of the other decisions in my life.

BEYOND THE GATES OF SPLENDOR

Splendor is not how I would have described my life. Magnificent just didn't come to mind when I looked at my situation. When I got to the halls of Alcoholics Anonymous, I was beat up and in bad shape. I was worn down, broken, lost, depressed, scared, and any other adjective you can come up with that describes a depleted life. I would have given anything for a life, a day, or even a moment of splendor and was just hoping to survive another day. There were times I didn't even want to survive another day. The alternative seemed easier.

After spending some time in AA, and staying off the drugs and alcohol, some of the fog started to clear. I noticed that other people had stories that paralleled my life, yet they were happy, joyous, and free. They seemed to have progressed beyond their problem. I wanted what they had and just staying sober was producing some results. I got a sponsor, I worked the steps, I went to meetings, and I didn't drink in between. Life started getting increasingly better. The wreckage of my past was clearing up. Splendor was in sight! I could see the gates.

Today, I consider myself a solid member of Alcoholics Anonymous and not just a participant. As I continue in my sobriety, helping others along the way, I find that I am catapulted beyond the gates of splendor, and I am afforded a wonderful life that I could not have imagined.

ATTITUDE OF GRATITUDE

By the time I finally quit drinking, I had absolutely nothing to be grateful for. I know my problems were of my own making, but that didn't make them any less real. My attitude wasn't necessarily ungrateful, but I definitely did not have an attitude of gratitude. My marriage was destroyed. My business was destroyed. My reputation was destroyed, and my spirit was destroyed. Heck, my whole life was basically destroyed. I had lots of dark attitudes: pity, sorrow, anger, fear, loneliness, poverty, shame, guilt, and even resentment.

My life showed it. As long as I had a negative attitude about anything, my life could not be filled with positive things. I could still feel the YUCK inside of me. When I heard "attitude of gratitude," it impressed me. Because I knew these other people in meetings had been where I was, yet they were grateful for so much.

I finally realized that I had plenty to be grateful for, and maybe by focusing on that, like the others said, it would help. I was grateful to be alive, and I was grateful to be free—well, kind of free. I still had a lot of hoops to jump through. I was grateful for the hope found in the promises—hope that my life could get better, and that nothing lost couldn't be restored.

If it was in God's will, it will be restored. I was grateful for a Higher Power that was in charge, and always had my best interests at heart, lifting a huge weight off my shoulders, making it easy to have an attitude of gratitude.

SEVEN DAYS WITHOUT A MEETING MAKES ONE WEAK.

That's WEAK, not WEEK, and it really is true. Occasionally, I have circumstances that cause me to go over a week without making it to a meeting. It's by choice. I realize that because if I really wanted to go, there is always a meeting that can be found, but nonetheless, occasionally I allow it to happen.

I work a good program. I never get an urge. I just get busy and overscheduled, and I never notice it to affect me, but my wife does. It seems like my whole attitude and outlook upon life will change backwards. I don't necessarily feel weaker. I don't recognize the subtle changes, which evidently aren't so subtle, but I'm quicker to judge, slower to overlook, lacking in grace, and questionable on mercy. Basically, I'm drained.

I need to not only fellowship with the members who have become my family, but I need to hear the experience, strength, and hope of the speakers in the meetings. I need to be filled back up—which means I need to be in meetings and seven days without a meeting makes one weak.

AA—ALIVE AGAIN

Boy is that the truth! Alive again! But for years, I couldn't imagine life without alcohol. To me, it was just part of everyday living. Life wouldn't be much without alcohol. No beer frames in bowling, no ice chest in the dugout during softball, and no drinks around the fire when camping. That sounded like death to me. After a long time living with daily drinking, things started to change. I found myself drinking even when I didn't want to.

I would miss scheduled events. I would plan family outings, only to cancel them later, either because of some other event that included drinking or drugging would take precedence, or often because I was just too loaded to make it. I had lost control of my life. I swear I was drinking against my will. It was controlling me and my life. People would say that drinking would lead to one of three places—jail, institutions, or death. I had already hit two of the three, and frankly, death wasn't sounding so bad. I pretty much felt dead already, and actual death often sounded less painful.

Alcoholics Anonymous changed everything. My entire attitude and outlook on life was transformed. As I stayed sober and worked the steps, my eyes, my heart, my mind, and my very soul became renewed. As I offered myself to God and got to know my Higher Power, I was reborn into a brand-new family. I was alive again!

THOUGHTS THAT KEEP ME SOBER

PRINCIPLE 10
PERSEVERANCE

My brethren, count it all joy when you fall into various trials. (James 1:2)

OVERINVEST IN THE TRIALS OF LIFE.

I've never failed; I've just found lots of ways that didn't work. So, I move on and try a different way. Eventually, I will accomplish my task and chalk up another success. If I don't go through the necessary trials, I will never succeed at my task.

Life is like that for me. I'm not always sure of what will produce the proper outcome. I just know that if I don't do something, I can't move forward. Going through the necessary trials of life sharpens my focus and understanding. It's the trials of life that not only give me direction, but also train me on what just doesn't work in life.

Life doesn't work well for me as a thinker only. I need to be a doer of life. Spending too much time in my head, trying to decipher my next successful move in life, doesn't usually work well for me. I end up lost in a bad neighborhood, but stepping out in action, faithfully doing the next indicated thing, tends to work.

When I simply continue to move forward, and overinvest in the trials of life, even though I may hit a lot of bumps in the road, I successfully end up at my destination. I end up there wiser and better off than I was just sitting and thinking about what to do. I conquer demons when I overinvest in the trials of life.

PRINCIPLE 10—PERSEVERANCE

DON'T GET TOO WELL BY THURSDAY.

I used to do this all the time. I would get so plastered on the weekends that Monday morning was spent swearing off alcohol. The sickness would last two to three days, and by Thursday, I would be feeling fine. I was well enough to start planning another weekend of the same things again. Every time, I would tell myself, "This time will be different," but it never was. It was always the same. Grief, heartache, headaches, demoralization, and a further deteriorated life were always the result. Wow, what a blast!

I seemed to have a built-in forgetter (and I still do). I wanted to party so much that I didn't care about all the bad that came with and after it. Once I was well, I thought I could alter the results for the next time, yet I never could. If I felt on Fridays the way I did on Mondays, I wouldn't have wanted to go out and get stupid all over again. Sadly, I seemed to get too well by Thursday to stop the insanity of my mind, and there went my decision-making. I had no rational thought.

I need to remember how deadly drinking is to my life. I need to remember that the outcome is never favorable. I need to make sure I don't get too well by Thursday.

S.L.I.P.—STOPPED LIVING IN THE PROGRAM

Time and time again, I see people disappear from the meetings and wonder what happened. Time and time again, I see them come back and hear the exact same thing from every single one of them. They had a slip, which means they—Stopped Living in the Program.

At some point, they got complacent. They rested on their laurels. Meetings just took up too much time, and they were healthy again, so living life was something they could now navigate on their own. They stopped living in the program and started living in their own hearts and minds again. No time to help others with their sobriety because someone else could do that. They had arrived and were ready to get back to their lives.

How easily they had forgotten that their life, before the program of Alcoholics Anonymous, wasn't much worth living. In fact, it wasn't much of a life at all without the program. Away from the fellowship, they couldn't relate to people, and people certainly couldn't relate to them. It was the same with all of them that came back. There's something about an alcoholic that just doesn't seem to function appropriately without the stabilizing power of the program of Alcoholics Anonymous. Once you've started living it, you never need to stop living in the program. If you stay in the fellowship, you will not slip.

DON'T QUIT BEFORE THE MIRACLE HAPPENS.

I've never been to a bad meeting. I know everyone may think they have. Truly, if God is really in charge of my life, and I am letting Him direct my steps, then He knew in advance every AA meeting I would ever attend. So, there must be some purpose for even those meetings that don't go so well. I sit there, arms folded, thinking, *What miracle? This meeting sucks*, and I end up walking out early, receiving nothing.

But the thing I needed to hear could have been from the very next speaker or the night's last speaker. Maybe the miracle is after the meeting, while talking to someone one-on-one. Maybe the miracle isn't mine today. Maybe today, I'm supposed to hand out the miracle. I go to meetings truly anticipating a miracle, but if I don't feel it, I leave. That's not how it always works!

If I listen to the topic and other stories with a spirit of service always in my heart, when I speak, God can use that for someone else there. The miracle always happens, and sometimes, I don't see it right away. Sometimes, the miracle happens after the recipient has time for the knowledge to become understood.

I get to meetings early so I can fellowship and serve. I share my experience, strength, and hope during the meetings. I stay after to fellowship and serve, and every time, I walk away sober. Now that's truly a miracle in itself. Every meeting has something for someone. Be involved, and don't quit before the miracle happens.

BITTER OR BETTER?

Life had become pretty miserable at the end of my drinking. I was angry about everything. I was mad at my boss for letting me go. I was mad at my family for letting me down. I was mad at my friends for failing me. I was mad at the courts for judging me and not understanding that it wasn't my fault. I was mad at the police for constantly arresting me, creating more and more destruction in my life. I was even mad at the treatment centers for not healing me. After all, I had paid a small fortune for the seven treatment centers I had been to, and I was still an angry mess. Nobody was fixing me. They all just wanted me to stop drinking and drugging, and I was bitter.

In a meeting of Alcoholics Anonymous, I heard someone say that I didn't have to stay that way. I was told I had a choice. I was told that if I followed a few simple suggestions, life could get better. They said there would be some work to do, but if I did the suggested work, everything in my life would change. My relationships with employees, friends, family, police, and even the courts would all get better.

I followed the suggestions that were given to me in Alcoholics Anonymous, and I did the suggested work. My life, and every aspect of it, got better. The choice is yours. Do you want bitter or better?

S.L.I.P.—SOBRIETY LOSES ITS PURPOSE

Before getting sober, my life was a mess. I tried many times, and many ways, to straighten it out, but it only got worse. It was a pointless endeavor until I put down the alcohol. I needed my life back, and that just wasn't possible as long as I was drinking. After attempts on my own, trying everything I could think of, along with multiple stints in treatment, I ended up in the house of Alcoholics Anonymous.

There, I learned how to stay sober. I learned how to navigate life and live on life's terms. Being committed to the program, sobriety had a profound purpose for me. My life was finally back in order. No longer was every day filled with pain and sorrow. After years of being of no use to myself, or anyone else, I had become a productive member of society. I was actually helping others.

Many times, I would see someone come into the program of Alcoholics Anonymous, get their lives cleaned up and back on track, and then go back out. They felt like with everything okay in life, they could go back to their old lifestyle and drink without harm. They would have a S.L.I.P., which I think stands for, "Sobriety Loses Its Purpose

They seemed to forget how bad it was, or they forget how powerless they were. Their purpose for getting sober was so successful that they didn't realize it was the same purpose for staying sober. I stay in the halls of Alcoholics Anonymous and learn from their unfortunate choices. I don't believe I will ever slip, as long as I never allow sobriety to lose its purpose.

AA IS A PM PROGRAM
(PREVENTATIVE MAINTENANCE).

Do I need to do this in the morning or in the evening? Is this an AM program or a PM program? Do I need it all the time? Yes! I need it all the time, but it's definitely a PM program—PM as in Preventative Maintenance. I never know, day to day, what I'll be going through or what tools I'm going to need in relation to it. So, I'd better be prepared.

I've heard it said in meetings that we take what we need. I never know what I'm going to need, so I just take it all. I carry a giant toolbelt and constantly add things to it. As things go unused or unneeded in my life, they get removed from the belt to make room for the new things I learn. If I stop going to meetings, or hanging out in the fellowship, I stop learning new tools to fill that belt and end up unprotected.

Getting here was too hard! I'm not going through that fight again. Quite frankly, I don't think I could. So, I do the leg work of life. I go to meetings, do service work, have a sponsor, help others, and thank God, my Higher Power, every day for somehow finding a way to make someone as unworthy as me useful and productive for His purpose. I am truly blessed! Beyond blessed, because I work a PM program.

GETTING STARTED IN AA WAS LIKE THE "GREEN EGGS AND HAM" BOOK. I COULDN'T EAT THEM FOR A WHILE, BUT IT TURNS OUT, I LIKE THEM.

The simple wisdom I hear in meetings never stops helping me. I can relate to almost everything. At first, going to meetings was like "green eggs and ham." I didn't want anything to do with them. I went because too many forces compelled me to go, but I didn't want to be there. I certainly didn't want to join the little club and partake of any sort of fellowship. I don't like green eggs and ham!

After staying sober for a while, I started hearing things that were being said. Before long, I could understand some of it. One thing was certain, almost everything I heard, I could relate to. Oh, I was different, but so were all these people. I kind of felt like I belonged.

I started getting involved and found that I enjoyed fellowship with others that had similar struggles as I did—especially since they seemed to have a solution! I have learned to follow suggestions and quit demanding that things go my way. I have learned to take care of my side of the street. I have learned to stay involved and remain a part of the fellowship. As it turns out, I do like green eggs and ham!

STAY IN THE HERD.

This is possibly the best advice I ever got. I don't think there's a safer place to be, especially if you are in the middle of the herd. Around the time I was getting sober, I was spending a lot of time sitting with my grandson watching TV. He used to love watching Animal Planet, which is a National Geographic show about different kinds of animals and creatures. The one thing I used to notice was how vulnerable the animals on the outside of the herd were.

It didn't matter what type of animal herd it was, or what type of predator it was, the stragglers on the outside of the herd were the only ones that were ever caught. Never did I see an animal from the middle of the herd get taken out. They were insulated from the predators. When I heard someone say, "Stay in the herd," a vivid picture of Animal Planet appeared in my mind. It made crystal-clear sense.

If I didn't want to get taken out by the predators in my life, I needed to stay in the herd. The closer to the middle of the herd, the safer it was. At that moment, I committed myself to paying attention, getting involved, and staying in the herd. I have been safe ever since, regardless of what predators came my way.

THE BIG BOOK IS A TEXTBOOK; IT'S MEANT TO STUDY, NOT JUST READ.

Have you ever watched a movie a second time? It amazes me the things I notice that I had missed the first time I saw it. Books are the same way for me. I spent an unfortunate amount of time behind bars, and although I hated to read, I got good at it. It was a way to make time pass and it gave me a view, or a vision, that was different than my four walls. It broke up the monotony.

As I was in and out of jail, I would periodically come across a book I had already read but found that nothing else sounded fun to read, so I'd read it again. It never disappointed me. I would always see something I had missed. It would cause an "aha moment," even though my first reading hadn't missed anything. So, while reading *The Big Book*, our basic text for Alcoholics Anonymous, one time through would be better than not reading it at all, but it's really more of a textbook to be studied. And every time you go through it, you will get something new and helpful.

God never ceases to amaze me. I think He does this on purpose. He knows who we are when we get here and just what shape we're in, so God gives us a little at a time, and only what we can handle. If we get more than we are ready for, too much information too fast, we may get overwhelmed and retain too little, or worse yet—relapse! But if I use *The Big Book* as a study guide for life, I constantly reap more benefits from the literature. I also increase my ability to be of service to God, and to be used for whatever He deems necessary in His service to His people.

GOD WILL DO
WHAT WE "COULD NOT" DO OURSELVES,
NOT WHAT WE "WOULD NOT" DO OURSELVES.

Faith without works is dead. *The Big Book* of Alcoholics Anonymous tells us that. So, when I read the Ninth Step Promises of Alcoholics Anonymous, and it says, "God is doing for us what we could not do ourselves," I can see the implication that I am supposed to be doing something.

I can't sit around and rest on the fact that I quit drinking and expect God to miraculously fix all my issues. My part must be done by me. Nobody else, not even God, is going to accomplish for me those things that I can accomplish myself. As I put out the effort, as I work on my shortcomings, there will inevitably be some things that I can't overcome on my own.

As I reach out for help from others in the program, continuing to do my work, even their help will sometimes not be enough. That's when God steps in to catapult me across the finish line. When my sincere effort isn't enough, God does for me what I am not capable of doing myself, despite my efforts. However, I must put out the effort. He is not going to do for me what I would not try to do myself, but He will do for me what I can't do myself.

LIVE ONE DAY AT A TIME AND SET GOALS. HOW DO THEY GO TOGETHER?

My goal was to have sustained sobriety, so when I came into Alcoholics Anonymous and heard that I needed to take life one day at a time, I was confused. How do you set a goal for the future and not live towards it? I didn't want to be sober just for a day. I wanted to be sober for the rest of my life. That was my goal, and you couldn't convince me that it wasn't a good one.

To work towards that end was a necessity or I was never going to get there. What I've learned, though, is that I can't get to my goal, any goal, immediately. Most goals are achieved in increments. A series of small advances, minor accomplishments, and quick goals that when I string them together, move me towards that larger goal I've set my sights on.

When it comes to sobriety, it was actually a huge accomplishment to get there just one day. It had been pretty much impossible to do that in the past. As I added a second day, and then a third, it started to make sense. Setting goals and living one day at a time actually work really well together. As I secure the success of a single day, stacking one on top of the other, I find myself steadily moving forward toward that sustained sobriety I've set my sights on.

STICK WITH THE WINNERS.

When I got to Alcoholics Anonymous, everyone was a winner compared to me. I was told that I had to change one thing—everything. How was I to know who the winners were? Some of the people in the program who had substantial clean time still had pretty screwed up lives. They were unhappy and displayed no signs of joy. That's certainly not what I would consider a winner.

Some of the people in the program didn't have much clean time, so I couldn't be sure if they were winners or not. Some came in and out of the program and had a lot of knowledge, but no success. Those didn't seem to be winners either. However, some of the people in the program seemed to have joy, even when their lives weren't always happy.

They seemed to be the ones that had worked the steps, the ones who followed "How It Works." They had sponsors, and they helped others. They were the people who did service work, not just in the program, but in their everyday lives as well. They were the ones who were seen on a regular basis at meetings and were usually attentive regarding newcomers. These were the ones that had something I wanted, something I deeply desired. They were the ones that didn't come in-and-out of the program; they just stayed. I wanted to be a winner, not just a survivor, so I chose to stick with the winners, and it worked!

PRINCIPLE 10—PERSEVERANCE

RECOVERY IS PROGRESSIVE, JUST LIKE ALCOHOLISM IS PROGRESSIVE.

I'm pretty sure I was an alcoholic from my very first drink, and I just didn't know it. In fact, I didn't even know what an alcoholic was. All I did know was that something happened when I tasted it, and I wanted more. It wasn't the taste I wanted more of, or the feeling it gave me the next day, it was the immediate rush of confirmation that everything was okay. It fixed every aspect of feelings I had. Life was going to be just fine. I had found the cure.

As I continued in life, problems came, but the alcohol soon washed them away. After a while, the problems became more than alcohol could wash away. In fact, alcohol wasn't working at all. It seemed that every time I drank, things got worse, not better. My cure had become a liability. I was stuck in my alcoholism and didn't even know it happened or where to turn.

I ended up joining a meeting of Alcoholics Anonymous. I'm pretty sure I was in recovery from my very first meeting, I just didn't know it. In fact, I didn't even know what recovery was. All I did know was that something happened while I was there, and I didn't want to drink. I couldn't explain it, but while in the presence of others in the meeting, the compulsion to drink subsided. The pain wasn't as strong while there, and as I continued to go, it almost felt like everything was going to be OK. Sobriety allowed my feelings to come back. Life was going to be just fine. I may not have found a cure, but I have found recovery, and I continue that in life. Every day gets easier and better as my recovery progresses.

IF I DON'T DRINK, I WON'T GET DRUNK.

Sounds simple, right? The halls of Alcoholics Anonymous are filled with people who struggle to get this simple concept. They do not want to get drunk, but not drinking never crossed their minds. They change the amount or type of alcohol, and their life still spirals downhill.

They stop hanging out with some of their "worse off" friends or stop going to some of these "more questionable" places, and their life STILL spirals downhill. They may even come to AA to fix their lives, and they still end up drunk.

There's a lot of things to do to straighten out a life that has been run ragged from alcohol, and it will take some work to do it, but before you can ever get any headway on fixing your life, you must first put down the alcohol. I can promise you this—if you don't drink, you won't get drunk!

AA IS NOT SOMETHING I JOINED, IT'S SOMETHING I LIVE.

That statement pretty much says it all for me. Yes, I did join Alcoholics Anonymous, but it has become far more than a simple club I belong to. It has become the lifestyle I've chosen to live. After attending meetings for a while, I saw many who had joined end up back out of the fellowship, with lives spiraling downhill. They had come to meetings, experienced something special, and tried to live life on their terms with what they had supposedly learned. It seems they hadn't incorporated the AA program into their daily life, and that just doesn't work.

I know I'm an alcoholic, and there's a lot of personal responsibility that comes with that knowledge. Like with any other disease, I can't address it when I'm in the hospital, or with my doctor, and then forget about it when I'm out and about living my life. Likewise, I can't address my alcoholism when I'm in a meeting, or with my sponsor, and then forget about it when I'm out and about living my life. I can't simply join the program, and then not live the program.

My life tends to be what I live out, not what I know. Keeping that thought at the forefront of my mind helps me to live out a life of sobriety that continues to be useful for my own growth and well-being, as well as allowing me to be of service to others. I am grateful that I've learned to live AA, as opposed to simply joining it.

IT'S NO LONGER A MESS, IT'S A MESSAGE.

My life was an absolute mess. To any normal person, it was unfixable. It's not just that I was hopeless; straightening out the mess my life had become also seemed hopeless. There was no way to get back to where I was, back to anything remotely resembling sanity. Normal was done and would never be seen again. I wonder if that's how Noah felt.

The first mention of alcohol in the Bible is of Noah being a drunkard. He is depicted as a black-out drunk. Yet, it is his family that God spared when the earth flooded. Noah, possibly the first registered alcoholic, was used to build the boat that saved life on earth. People thought he was crazy, and he quite possibly was. Most of us alcoholics tend to have that crazy gene.

As I look around the halls of Alcoholics Anonymous, I see lots of crazies, and I love watching God use and transform them. Noah may have been a mess but look at the message he became. It wasn't till after the flood that we see him as a black-out drunk. However, if he knew how to make wine after the flood, logic would insinuate he knew before the flood. His alcoholism probably hadn't progressed that far yet.

I'm only speculating, but I see it in the halls of AA regularly. The prior mess of my life has been used as a message to others. Just as God used the story of Noah to show how man cannot live an upright life without Him, God has used the mess of my life as a message to others of the hope we have in Him. My life is no longer a mess; it's a message.

WHEN YOU WALK WITH GOD, YOU ALWAYS REACH YOUR DESTINATION.

I love having a Higher Power to direct my steps. Left to my own devices, I'm not the smartest guy on the block. When I head out on my own, I tend to get lost. So, I don't blindly set out about my day any longer. I always pause before starting my day and ask God what our plans are.

You see, I never head out anywhere alone. I no longer walk through life on my own power and ability. I walk through life with God, because He knows better than I do, what I'm supposed to do, and where in life I'm supposed to go. I start my day in prayer, asking my Higher Power to guide me.

If I pay attention, life doesn't just flutter by, it actually has purpose woven into almost everything that I do. I don't always recognize it at first, but when I allow my path to be guided, instead of running through life half-cocked, I always reach my destination, even when I'm not sure what that destination is.

No matter what project is before me, I know now I never have to approach it alone. Besides all the angels that have been charged to watch over me today, I also walk with God. Therefore, I can be sure, I will always reach my destination.

I GO TO MEETINGS TO SEE WHAT HAPPENS TO PEOPLE WHO STOP GOING TO MEETINGS.

The truth is, I go to meetings for a lot of reasons; my own sobriety, to be there for another alcoholic, and even sometimes, just to get out of the house are some of them. On the other hand, to see what happens to people who stop going is huge. I didn't know to look for that when I first became acquainted with this organization that has impacted millions since it was founded in 1935. I thought you were either in the program, or you were not.

After spending many years in the halls of Alcoholics Anonymous, I noticed some of the people disappear. Did they move? Did they find a different meeting they like better? Did they fall back into their addiction to suffer all over again? In time, the answer was apparent. Over and over again, I'd see some of those who had disappeared show back up in the meetings. Time and time again, I'd hear them say it didn't get better; it only got worse.

Not once did I see someone come back into the program of Alcoholics Anonymous and say, "Hey guys, after stopping for a bit, I now have control." It was always the same. Abstinence was still the only thing that worked for them. Unfortunately, my mind doesn't always stay in perfect form, and I can rest on my laurels if I'm not careful. Going to meetings and seeing what has happened to those who stopped going to meetings reminds me of how dangerous and powerful my addictions are. I pray I never tire of meetings.

PRINCIPLE 10—PERSEVERANCE

GO TO A MEETING WHEN YOU WANT TO GO. GO TO A MEETING WHEN YOU DON'T WANT TO GO.

The point is, just go to a meeting. I can honestly say that it works for me every time. Every single time I go to a meeting, I get recentered and refocused, even when I didn't want to go. Sometimes, it's in big ways, and sometimes, it's in little ways, but it's always in a positive way.

I'm not sure if it's working with others, or if it's others working with me. I'm not sure if it's the getting out of myself and sharing or the contemplating and growth from listening to someone else share. Maybe, it's just the simple fellowship with others who have become my family. What I do know is this, my life goes better when I go to meetings. Whether I'm excited to go, or reluctant to go, it's always better when I go.

I think I actually get more out of the ones I don't feel like going to. My Higher Power tends to use me when I submit to His will and go when I don't want to or don't feel like it. When I stretch myself and step out of my comfort zone, I allow God to stretch me and mold me into the vessel He can best use for His purposes. Therefore, I go to a meeting when I want to, and I go to a meeting when I don't want to. I just go when I'm called to.

IF YOU WALK TEN MILES INTO THE FOREST, DON'T BE SURPRISED IF IT TAKES TEN MILES TO WALK OUT.

It sounds pretty logical, right? Yet we live in a world where we not only want instant gratification, but we also demand it. So, why should it be any different with our sobriety? If we decide not to drink, shouldn't we instantly be sober? Why doesn't our decision alone provide the necessary ingredients for sustained sobriety?

I'm pretty sure I was an alcoholic the moment I had my first taste of that magic elixir, but I wasn't actually drinking alcoholically. Although I often longed for the next opportunity to get hammered, it wasn't something I had to do every day. Over time, the obsession won over, and I couldn't get through a day without alcohol. The insanity didn't happen overnight, but in time, it came.

When I came to a point where I couldn't take it anymore and decided to put the bottle down, I'm pretty sure I was in recovery from that first day. That didn't immediately remove the insanity or the obsession. I soon realized that to accomplish that, actively working on my recovery was going to have to become part of my daily life.

I joined Alcoholics Anonymous and participated in the program just as fervently as I had participated in my addiction. In time, I came out of the pain and suffering and into the light of sobriety. So, if you walk ten miles into the forest, don't be surprised if it takes ten miles to walk out.

PRINCIPLE 10—PERSEVERANCE

TIME TAKES TIME.

When I came into the program of Alcoholics Anonymous, I couldn't fathom years of sobriety. First, who could possibly go an entire life without alcohol? Second, who would want to? The problems I was having in my life gave credence to the fact that I had to quit drinking, but I had no idea how to accomplish it.

I kept hearing that it was one day at a time, but I needed to do more than one day. I had been to seven inpatient treatments, and I had gotten sober for one day, four days, and thirty days. I was even in one for fifty-four days. Every time, I was drunk within three days of getting out of treatment. One day doesn't work; I need more time, lots more! Then, it hit me.

It's not one day; it's one day at a time. Time takes time, and if I want more of it, I must start with today first. If I can stay sober today, I'll have hope for tomorrow. By getting a sponsor who could guide me through the program and hanging out in the fellowship on a regular basis, time has added up. One day at a time turned into sixteen years later. Now, I'm looking back and thinking, *Wow, how did this happen?*

I just quit drinking for one day, and that brought me to a second day. Then, I quit drinking for one day, and that brought me to a third. Today, I have over sixteen years of sobriety, and it didn't just happen; it took time, but I only had to stay sober one day, over and over and over again.

IT ISN'T A CRUTCH; IT'S A PROSTHETIC.

Alcoholics Anonymous has been referred to as a crutch by some people in my life. I'm not really sure if that's a bad thing, although I know that's how they mean it. Personally, I think it's their way of justifying their own lack of ability to address their own drinking issues.

Calling it a crutch has a bit of truth to it. I lean on Alcoholics Anonymous to support me in my times of difficulty. When I have trouble walking through life, I guess you could say I use the crutch of AA to help me take those steps. *The Big Book* of Alcoholics Anonymous says that we alcoholics are like people who have lost their legs. We can never grow them back again. Likewise, I'm an alcoholic and can never be a non-alcoholic again. Just as a person who has lost a leg may need a crutch to walk through life, as an alcoholic, I need AA to walk through life.

Calling it a crutch, though, doesn't accurately depict its importance or its ability. While a crutch may help a one-legged person, a prosthetic is a lot closer to having one's leg back. We may not be able to grow a new leg, but we can replace it with one that achieves the function. Alcoholics Anonymous has allowed me to function as a normal member of society. In fact, not just a normal member, but a productive member. You would never know I have the disease of alcoholism as I walk through life, because of what God, the members of Alcoholics Anonymous, and the program of Alcoholics Anonymous has done in my life. It isn't a crutch; it's a prosthetic.

GRIND DOWN THE MOUNTAINTOPS
AND FILL IN THE VALLEYS.

Living life sober is a constant work in progress. My life before sobriety consisted of mountains that were too high to climb over, and valleys that were too low to climb out. It was a constant rollercoaster of ups and downs with no serenity in sight. People say we make mountains out of molehills, but trying to get over one was like climbing a mountain. If it was a molehill, I could kick it out of the way, but that wasn't the case. Some may have started as molehills, but they had become mountains.

Before I could get over one, I needed to eliminate the peaks. I needed to get them down to something manageable. As far as the valleys in my life, they had become so low that it was like there was a mountain on each side. They needed to be filled in some, so I could at least see the top of the hole I was trying to crawl out of.

My rollercoaster of life had become unmanageable. The mountains were too high, and the valleys were too low. I needed to start somewhere, and reducing the burden was my only hope. I was given some good advice. I was told to grind down the mountaintops and fill in the valleys. Getting where I wanted to go couldn't be done all at once, but as long as I continued to move forward in sobriety, the mountains got smaller, and the valleys weren't as deep. Life still has speed bumps and dips in the road, but the mountains and valleys have all but disappeared.

IT WORKS IF YOU WORK IT.

You can't sit around thinking about a different way of life and expect it to materialize. Just because you believe it can be better, just because you believe you can change, doesn't mean it's going to happen by osmosis. Faith without works is dead. You must act if you want results.

I heard a good story in treatment, and it goes like this: "Three frogs were sitting on a lily pad, and two frogs decided to jump off the lily pad. How many frogs were left on the lily pad?" Seems easy enough, the answer is one, right? Wrong! Three were left on the lily pad. Two decided to jump off, but never did anything, so, they were still on the lily pad. To me, it sounded a bit corny, but it really does work if you work it.

The first sentence of "How It Works" says, "Rarely have we seen a person fail who has thoroughly followed our path." Once that hit me, I realized that was the work I needed to do. Follow the path of the conquerors that went before me. Read the book. Work the steps. Go to meetings. Have a sponsor. Help when you are asked and get a service position. Do every responsible thing suggested in, "How It Works." One thing I can promise you, it truly does work if you work it!

PRINCIPLE 10—PERSEVERANCE

IT TAKES A LONG TIME
FOR THE SWELLING TO GO DOWN.

My head was pretty big in life. I always thought I was something more than what I was. After all, we're not supposed to go through life depressed, looking down on ourselves, and claiming to be failures. Aren't we taught to have a positive attitude and a can-do outlook on our goals? It only seems logical that the more I believe in myself, the better my performance in life will be. Society tells us that we have no limitations except the ones we put on ourselves. We can do anything we put our minds to. The only thing that can stop us is our own failure to try.

Even if I look at the biblical point of view, doesn't the Bible say I'm a child of God? Doesn't it say I'm part of a royal priesthood, a chosen people, and created in His image? I can do all things, right? So, how do I keep from getting a big head? I am something special. Putting that to the test, holding on to my greatness, I was able to muster up just enough success to land myself a seat in Alcoholics Anonymous. My greatest achievement was realizing that I'm an alcoholic.

It's true, the Bible says, "I can do all things," but it goes on to say, "Through Christ, who gives me strength" (Ph. 4:13 NKJV, NLT). In Alcoholics Anonymous, I came to learn who I really am. I'm a flawed individual that needs a Power greater than myself to restore me to sanity. That's right, on my own, I'm insane. I'm a big-headed person who thinks my accomplishments are my own. They're not. Without His help, I can do nothing worthy. I'm simply a vessel that He uses if I let Him. Thinking I'm something more than I am isn't such a problem today. But it took a long time for the swelling to go down.

THOUGHTS THAT KEEP ME SOBER

PRINCIPLE 11

PATIENCE

Therefore humble yourselves under the mighty hand of God, that He may exalt you in due time, casting all your care upon Him, for He cares for you. Be sober, be vigilant; because your adversary the devil walks about like a roaring lion, seeking whom he may devour. (1 Peter 5:6-8)

RARELY AND SOUGHT—
THE FIRST AND LAST WORDS IN
"HOW IT WORKS"

There's a lot of information between the first and last words of "How It Works," and we need every bit of it. Fused together, they describe why most alcoholics don't make it to sobriety—RARELY SOUGHT! Look at the facts. Just over one million copies of *The Big Book* are sold worldwide each year.

Last year, just in the United States, domestic beer alone sold 141.55 billion barrels with 162 12oz bottles in each barrel. That's more than my calculator would compute. We are losing, but not all those drinkers are alcoholics, and they're not all our problem. I am way more than one in a million, and I'm fortunate, no, blessed, to be one of the lucky ones.

Not everybody makes it. Most don't even seek it out. However, if we separate the two words (rarely and sought) and add "How It Works," in between, then they become life blood to the recovering alcoholic. In the first part, "rarely" have we seen a person fail who has thoroughly followed our path. "arely" tells us that, if we do what we are taught, we will not fail. In the last part, "God could and would, if He were sought." The word "sought" tells us that God will see us through if we seek Him. Embrace the first and last words, and follow everything in between.

MORE WILL BE REVEALED.

When I first got sober, I was as confused as one could be. *Is this it, I thought, no more fun and excitement? A life destined to be boring and deprived of joy, stuck in meeting rooms filled with other degenerates who had destroyed their lives too?* With no clear vision of tomorrow, how could I even do it?

I hung around anyway, knowing that I had tried everything else. In time, life started to settle down. I began learning things about myself, as well as learning things about sobriety. Going to meetings of Alcoholics Anonymous was kind of like going to school. Every meeting was like another class, filled with lots of teachers. Some good teachers who had been in this University for years and other teachers who were pretty new. All of them seemed to have something I could learn from though.

The longer I stayed, the easier life was to deal with. As time went on, I learned more about navigating life's challenges. Pretty soon, I found myself teaching others. Although I was confused and doubtful when I first came into the program, the solution was eventually revealed. If you're new to Alcoholics Anonymous, don't be discouraged. Be consistent, and more will be revealed.

PROGRESS, NOT PERFECTION.

Boy, does that three-word phrase make me feel better! Progress is hard enough, but perfection is impossible. As long as I keep moving forward, though, I'll be OK. Life in recovery seems to go in spurts for me. I feel like I'm standing still sometimes, stagnant in my recovery, and then suddenly, there's this burst of progress. I guess that's what it means in the Step Nine promises, where it says "Sometimes quickly and sometimes slowly."

It might feel like I'm not moving forward, but as long as I'm continuing to work the program, going to meetings, fellowshipping with others, helping the ones in need, and so on, life progresses. Sometimes, it doesn't happen as fast as I'd like, but at other times, faster than I could have ever imagined. Not every day brings forth that feeling of success while I'm living it, yet at the end of the day, when I look back over those hours, I find I haven't gone backwards, and that in itself is progress for me.

I no longer go to bed in tears of despair due to the life I'm living. Now, I often go to bed with tears of gratitude for the life I have been given. It's progress, not perfection, and that has become my daily expectation.

ONE DAY AT A TIME

When it comes to drinking, or should I say, when it comes to trying not to drink, this advice got me through many times. Quitting drinking forever can seem overwhelming, but just for today, I can stay sober fairly easy. I can go to a meeting or make myself busy for any twenty-four-hour period far easier than quitting for the rest of my life. One day at a time helps. In fact, sometimes it's one hour at a time.

I don't have to get all worked up about never being able to drink again. I just have to get all worked up about the struggle to stay sober today. One day at a time. Yesterday is gone, and tomorrow isn't here yet. The one is unchangeable; the other will have its own troubles. Today is all I have to be concerned about. The meetings, the fellowship, the literature, and the steps keep me sober, one day at a time.

PATIENCE IS NOT THE ABILITY TO WAIT; IT IS THE ABILITY TO KEEP A GOOD ATTITUDE WHILE YOU WAIT.

Some things just take time, so waiting is inevitable. Does that mean I'm being patient at those times? Anyone who knows me could answer that with a resounding, "NO." I may be better than I was a few years ago, but I'm a doer, not a thinker.

In being a doer, I want to progress forward. Staying in motion is simply more comfortable than waiting. Waiting feels like I am wasting time. I can't move forward while waiting around for something, anything at all. Nonetheless, waiting is inevitable at times. It's something I often have no control of.

How I deal with the waiting, though, that's something I can control. My thoughts, my feelings, and my attitude are all things that are on my side of the street. Those are all my responsibility. How I perceive a situation, and how I react to it, are greatly affected by my attitude.

That attitude affects my feelings, and then my feelings manipulate my thoughts. Suddenly, my waiting, even if it's on something good, has spiraled me into an impatient screwball. Angst fills me, and serenity disappears, so patience is a necessity. When I'm faced with having to wait on something, it's my attitude towards it that must be guarded. Only then, do I really have patience.

KNOWLEDGE IS KNOWING WHAT TO SAY WHEN YOU OPEN YOUR MOUTH. WISDOM IS KNOWING IF YOU SHOULD OPEN IT.

Knowledge and wisdom have both escaped me in the past. When I opened my mouth, I never worried if I knew what to say, I just said what I wanted. Whether it hurt someone, sounded stupid, made someone angry, or anything else wasn't my concern. The fact that I wanted to say it was all that mattered.

As far as knowing if I should open my mouth or not was easy. If I wanted to, I should. The feelings or thoughts of others didn't matter much to me. I was arrogant, egotistical, self-centered, and rather narcissistic. Life was about me, my desires, my thoughts, and my ways, period. You could join me or get the hell out of my way.

Thank God, I've changed! Thank God, I've grown, and thank God I've learned! Now, before I open my mouth, I think about what I'm going to say. I make sure I know what it is I should be saying, and I make a decision whether I should even say it. Life is no longer simply about me and my desires. Life is about my service to others.

Oh, I still take care of myself, and often before I take care of others, but knowledge and wisdom are important to me now. I still tend to be opinionated, but I'm conscious of what those opinions are. I try to use a kind of "God consciousness" before spouting off my thoughts. When I do this, my thoughts tend to have value, and my decisions make sense.

I used to think knowledge was just knowing something, and wisdom was understanding it. Seeing more clearly now, I prefer to think of knowledge as knowing what to say when I open my mouth, and wisdom as knowing if I should open it.

IT'S A LIFE SENTENCE.

I hear people ask, "How long do I have to keep going to meetings?" The general answer is, "Just cut back until you get loaded, then you will know." The point is, for most of us, the one thing we've had in common, if we went back out, is that we quit going to meetings. Your disease isn't going away. If you're an alcoholic, if you have our disease of alcoholism, then you have it for life. There is no cure.

We must keep our disease in remission, and we do that by staying active in the treatment of our disease. Not only is our disease a life sentence, but so is the solution. We can hold our disease at bay indefinitely. Unlike some other life sentence diseases, ours doesn't have to result in death. All we must do is follow a few simple suggestions. All we must do is stay in the fellowship, which IS the treatment for our disease.

KNOWLEDGE SPEAKS,
BUT WISDOM LISTENS.

Knowledge is important! I don't learn much from those who have none. I can only share what I know; I certainly can't share something I don't know. Without some knowledge, I'm stifled in my assistance and service to others. On the other hand, if I'm constantly acquiring knowledge without taking time to gain perspective and sound judgment, then I simply know stuff. If my knowledge is not cultivated, then I will never gain wisdom.

Without wisdom, I am incomplete in my ability to teach my knowledge to others. I lose the perspective that experience brings. Knowledge by itself is better than no knowledge at all, but knowledge doesn't translate to service without the wisdom of action.

God gave me one mouth and two ears. It seems my ears might be twice as important as my mouth is. I share my knowledge with my mouth by imparting to others, but I gain my wisdom by listening to those who know what I do not.

REACH FOR PERFECTION,
BUT BE HAPPY IF YOU JUST MAKE PROGRESS!

Boy, that statement is nice to hear. If perfection was necessary, we all might as well give up. Perfection is never going to happen till I arrive in heaven. I do, however, need to strive for perfection. That's how I progress in life. If my final goal is something actually achievable, what do I do when I get there? I constantly need to reach for a greater purpose, greater ability, or greater understanding. It's the reach up and forward that continues to advance me.

A series of small goals that move me towards my larger goals is how I find success. If I don't have attainable goals, frustration will set in, and I'll constantly feel like a failure. As I find success in the small goals, I'm propelled towards a higher one. Victory after victory breeds growth. I'm taught one day at a time, not just for the sake of having one day, but for the sake of having one success.

As I stacked the success of one day on top of the success of another day, and did that six times, I ended up with one week. As I stacked that on top of another week, about three times, I ended up with one month, all the time just focusing on the day I was currently living. I know that in life, I can never attain perfection, but as I try to, I find progress. This holds true for me, not just in sobriety, but in every aspect of my life. It's not about the arrival, it's about the journey, and that's progress, not perfection.

PRINCIPLE 11—PATIENCE

LEARN TO LISTEN; LISTEN TO LEARN.

God gave me one mouth and two ears. That must make hearing twice as important as talking. When I think about it, I never learned anything from talking, but boy, did I do a lot of it! I was always more interested in telling you what was on my mind than hearing what was on yours. Even when I tried to listen, I couldn't seem to hear or understand.

I still struggle with hearing, not because of any physical malady with my ears, but due to a wandering mind. It's as if I can only concentrate on what is being said for a short period.

I have had to learn how to listen in order to actually hear and understand others. I have to pay close attention when someone is speaking in order to really hear what it is they're saying, and that has been an incredible learning experience for me.

When I listen and understand, I learn. It's so simple and yet so amazing. I am constantly overwhelmed at how much life logically falls into place with a few simple truths that I learn when I listen. Now that I've learned to listen, I listen to learn.

IT'S A FREE GIFT!
ALL YOU HAVE TO DO IS EARN IT.

Sobriety costs nothing. It's free, but you can't get it by osmosis. If you're sitting on your couch doing nothing, sobriety isn't going to come and find you. If you have a drinking problem and don't realize it, or haven't admitted it, sobriety isn't going to happen.

Some gifts that are free actually require a little something from the receiving party before they can be given. You don't win a free gift from a drawing if you don't enter your name into the drawing to begin with. Free gifts that come with a purchase of something require you to earn the free gift by making a purchase first. Not to get all spiritual or anything, but the Bible teaches that salvation is a free gift from God, but even then, you have to accept Christ as your risen Savior before you can receive the free gift of God.

Well, it's kind of like that with sobriety. You must accept the fact that you are an alcoholic. You must surrender your life, as well as your will, to a Power greater than yourself. You must live in the solution and realize that it's not all about you.

LIVE EASY BUT THINK FIRST.

I was at a meeting held at an AA hall that I had not been to before, and the guy I went there with pointed to the five signs I see at most AA halls and said they were out of order. I looked at them, and I responded saying that I didn't know what order they were in. So he explained.

The five signs in their proper order should have been: "LIVE AND LET LIVE," "EASY DOES IT," "BUT FOR THE GRACE OF GOD," "THINK, THINK, THINK," and "FIRST THINGS FIRST." When placed accordingly, the first word in each of those five signs says, "LIVE EASY BUT THINK FIRST." Together, the five of them create a rather worthy approach.

First, I need to "LIVE" my life to the best of my ability, not getting wrapped up in judging others. Second, I need to take it "EASY," not getting too wound up and not taking on too much too fast. Third, I need to acknowledge that "BUT" for the grace of God, none of this would be possible. Fourth, I need to "THINK" what my motives are and whether it's the means to a good, bad, right, or wrong end. Fifth, I need to put "FIRST" those things that are the next indicated thing, not getting the cart ahead of the horse, so to speak. Enjoy life, live in the fellowship, and "LIVE EASY BUT THINK FIRST!"

IN THE END, IT WILL ALL BE OK, AND IF IT'S NOT OK, IT'S NOT THE END.

By the time I got to AA, nothing was OK. My working situation, my living situation, my marriage, and every other relationship, were all messed up or non-existent. I kept hearing people talk about how things got better, people who had stories that could have been my own. Things were OK for them.

They had lived lives as unmanageable as mine and found a way to overcome the destruction. They had the same mental obsession and physical addiction as me, the same disease, yet they were living with joy. I thought I was at the end, but it seemed that a new beginning could be found if I only knew the way.

The people in AA had a way, a solution, an actual blueprint of "How It Works," if you follow some simple steps, not necessarily easy, but simple, structured, practical suggestions that can be easily followed. I actually found hope again, and through the stories I continued to hear, my faith was built up.

It wasn't really the end. Everything was going to be OK. I got a sponsor. I worked the steps. I attended meetings regularly, and guess what, it's not even the end, and everything is already OK.

THE FOUR L'S—
LIVE, LISTEN, LOVE, AND LEARN

These four words show a blueprint of success. Fifteen years into my recovery, and I look back and see that this was an outline of progression in my life. My life had deteriorated to the point where I was simply existing. You couldn't really call what I was doing living. Counselors, lawyers, family, friends, police, pretty much everyone gave me advice, but no matter how hard I tried, I just couldn't concentrate enough to listen.

Self-absorbed, I loved myself, but I hated myself. I couldn't begin to love anyone or anything else, and learning was out of the question. I was barely existing. When I put down the bottle, and left it down, things gradually started to change, bit by bit. I began feeling things that I hadn't felt in years. Some good, some bad, but I could feel!

I was actually living again. As the fog cleared from my head and I continued to truly live, I started hearing those suggestions from others. The more I listened, the more I healed. I found myself OK in my own skin. In fact, I loved myself and respected myself. This enabled me to love others. As my love for others, and my service to others, grew, I found that I had a life I could have never imagined. I had learned to love, listen, and live!

IF YOU SIT IN A BARBERSHOP LONG ENOUGH, YOU'RE GOING TO GET A HAIRCUT.

When I first came to Alcoholics Anonymous, I was told that I shouldn't go to familiar places. I was told I shouldn't hang out with familiar people. Any place I used to drink or drug, I shouldn't go to! Anybody I used to drink or drug with, I shouldn't socialize with anymore. I came to understand that, if I hung around the same places, I would end up with the same results. If I hung out with the same crowd of people, I would do the same things.

The more I hung out at meetings, the more I recognized the similarities between myself and the others that were there. When I heard someone say, "If you sit in the barbershop long enough, you're going to get a haircut," it made perfect sense. I wanted to be sober, so I had to dissociate myself from the old places and people I used to associate with. After all, you don't go to a bar for a coke, and you don't go to a whore house for a kiss. I will become a part of the atmosphere I immerse myself in.

SOMETIMES, THE BEST THING TO DO IS NOTHING.

As good as that advice may be, that's just not my strong point. Doing nothing is difficult. I'm a fixer by nature. Sometimes, my wife wants to vent without me doing anything. She just wants to share the day she had, tell me the things that were a struggle, and get it out of her system.

I immediately set out to solve the problem, fix the issue, and make her life better. Wrong! She doesn't want anything from me but a listening ear. She'll even tell me that, and I still don't get it. On top of that, I never said I was a good fixer, and if her goal wasn't to have something fixed, how do I even know where to begin?

When I pray, I struggle to wait for the answer. I want to move forward and do what's necessary, and I have no idea what that is, because I haven't got the message yet. I tend to get the proverbial cart ahead of the horse. The Bible says if we wait for the Lord, our strength will be renewed.

If I'm feeling weak, maybe doing nothing is the smarter idea. I can act or react when my strength is restored. If I'm not sure how to address a situation, it might be best not to address it, rather than going off halfcocked. Taking action is good, as that is usually how we accomplish things in life, but sometimes the best thing to do is nothing.

H.A.L.T.—HUNGRY, ANGRY, LONELY, TIRED

Those are some of my most vulnerable times, when I'm hungry, angry, lonely, or tired. I struggle to think right most of the time, but when I'm vulnerable, it's almost impossible.

If I am hungry, I have a hard time focusing on anything. I feel like a car that is out of gas; I can't go anywhere or accomplish anything. If I am angry, my entire attitude tends to be in the toilet. I am short with, and judgmental toward, almost everybody. That anger comes out in all my actions. If I am lonely, I'm depressed. No man is an island, and that certainly rings true with me. God definitely didn't create me to be alone. It feels like death. If I am tired, I want to give up. I feel useless and unable to go on. Sometimes, that brings resentments, if I blame others for over-using me. Sometimes, it brings insecurity, if I feel unable to continue. At any rate, I have learned to overcome H.A.L.T. (hungry, angry, lonely, tired). I preemptively guard against them and avoid letting them come about in the first place.

If they do try to rise up, I have simple defenses against them. If I am hungry, I eat before doing anything else. That helps me avoid bad decisions. If I am angry, I pray. I make sure my side of the street is clear, and I let go. I'm the one it really hurts anyway. If I am lonely, I go to a meeting or hit up a friend. It soon reminds me that I never have to be alone. The fellowship is always available, and God is always with me. If I am tired, I rest. I pray. I go to church or do whatever it takes to fill me back up.

If I want to be productive in my life, I should refrain from too many actions when I am hungry, angry, lonely, or tired. If I am struggling with something, I first should check if I'm being affected by H.A.L.T. and address it accordingly if I am.

PRINCIPLE 11—PATIENCE

WHEN YOU'RE TEMPTED TO LOSE PATIENCE WITH SOMEONE, REMEMBER HOW PATIENT GOD HAS BEEN WITH YOU.

I want everyone I know who struggles with drugs and alcohol to come to Alcoholics Anonymous and recover from their addictions. Why can't they simply look at the changes I've made in my life, and see the difference it would make in theirs, if they got sober?

All the times I walked in and out of the halls of AA remind me that, at one point, I was just like that myself. God was so patient, and He never walked out on me. No matter how many times I gave up on myself, no matter how many times I turned away from His guiding hand, no matter how often I buried myself in addiction, whenever I turned to God, He was there, patiently waiting for me to quit abusing Him, countless others, and mostly myself.

When I think about that, it helps me to have hope for others. It helps me to have some semblance of patience with the ones I struggle with. Whether it's drug or alcohol related or some issues in life, whenever I find myself losing patience with someone, I remember how patient God has been with me, and I am able to impart grace instead of judgment.

GOOD MORNING, THIS IS GOD.
I WILL BE HANDLING ALL YOUR AFFAIRS TODAY,
AND I WON'T NEED YOUR HELP!
HAVE A GOOD DAY!

How in the world is God going to handle all my affairs if I don't tell Him what it is I need Him to do? Doesn't He, just like everybody else, need my input? That may sound ridiculous, but that's pretty much how I acted in the past. I had to have a say in everything, even if it had nothing to do with me.

One of the great things about being in the program of Alcoholics Anonymous is that I've learned I'm not responsible for everything. I have learned that it's not all about me and what I can figure out. All I really have to do is the next indicated thing that is set before me. Of course, I'll want guidance from my Higher Power, but God already knows what my needs are. He may need me to be attentive to His guidance, but He doesn't need me to worry about the details.

If I have taken my Third Step, and truly turned my life and will over to His care, then I need to trust that He will align things in a way that will benefit, not harm. It says in "How It Works" that there is One who has all power and that that One is God. What a relief it is to know that He will be handling all my affairs today.

When I think of me handling all my affairs on my own when God has all power, the choice is rather simple. That's exactly how I try to keep my program, simple, and it's got a lot easier to do with God in charge.

YESTERDAY IS HISTORY. TOMORROW IS A MYSTERY. YOU CAN ONLY LIVE IN TODAY.

Living in the past won't do me any good. Yesterday is gone. I can reminisce about the good things that used to be and end up drunk, drowning my sorrows, because life isn't good anymore. I can look at all the bad things that caused life to be like it is and end up drunk, feeling sorry for myself.

Living in tomorrow won't do me any good. Tomorrow isn't here yet. I could dream about what good things could come tomorrow, get anxious, and end up drunk, because they haven't happened yet. I could look at all the consequences left ahead, and how tough my life is going to be, and end up drunk from being overwhelmed with fear.

Today, I can do whatever I can do. I have some amount of control over today. I can take positive steps, move forward, and attempt to accomplish something today. Today, I can accomplish something. I can't accomplish something yesterday; it's gone. Today, I can try. Tomorrow, I can't accomplish anything; it's not here yet. I can only accomplish something in life today, because today is the only day I'm currently living in.

I can learn from yesterday, but it's gone. I certainly can't accomplish anything by dwelling in it. I can plan for tomorrow to some degree, but I don't know what tomorrow will bring, so I certainly can't live in it. Yesterday is history; tomorrow is a mystery. You can only live in today if you want to get anywhere.

GOD HOLD MY HAND, WATCH MY TONGUE, AND GUIDE MY FEET.

Sometimes it's, "God, hold my tongue, watch my feet, and guide my hand." At other times, it's "God, hold my feet, watch my hand, and guide my tongue." The point is, I can't do this without the help of my Higher Power.

I need God to hold my hand as I trudge the road of happy destiny. Honestly, I need Him to carry me some of the time. Not as much now as I needed early on, but it's God's hand that keeps me from falling.

I need God to watch my tongue as there is life and death in it. My tongue can bring condemnation and judgment upon me, as well as those He would prefer me to help. Without God's direction, my tongue causes trouble.

I need Him to guide my feet, so I don't step in a hole or fall off a cliff. He not only protects the steps that I take, but He also directs them. When I let God guide my feet, I always end up where He wants me to be. That enables me to do what He wants me to do and that brings joy!

There is something about following the will of my Creator, doing what He created me to do, that brings joy and gratitude that is unexplainable. It keeps me wanting more.

DON'T GIVE UP FIVE MINUTES BEFORE THE MIRACLE.

How many times have I done that? How many times have I got worn down and given up five minutes before my breakthrough? Never give up! You never know when your answer will come. You never know when your strength will arrive. You never know when you'll hear what you need to hear.

I can't count the number of times I have been in a meeting and heard somebody share about some type of pain or struggle that they were dealing with, and they were reaching out for help. Then I would hear somebody else share and I would think, *Man, that's just what that person needed to hear.* Then I'd look around and see that they had left and missed their solution.

As I was dwelling on that tragedy, I could remember many times that I, too, had been in a meeting and wasn't getting anything out of it, or I got bored and left. It made me wonder how many miracles I had missed. I heard somebody say in a meeting, "Don't leave five minutes before you need to hear what you need," and that's the same thing.

Don't give up five minutes before the miracle. If you are driven to do something, and it has come to you through rational thought, directed by your Higher Power, see it through to completion. You never know when the miracle will arrive.

IT'S BETTER TO KEEP SILENT AND BE THOUGHT A FOOL THAN TO SPEAK AND REMOVE ALL DOUBT.

This is an impossible task for me. Even after some time in sobriety, I still want to voice my opinion, whether I'm educated on the topic or not. It's like a curse. I'm taught to pray and meditate, prayer being talking to God, and meditation listening to Him. Guess what, I'm better at prayer. Go figure.

Fortunately, I've now been in recovery awhile, so not everything I say is foolish. However, when I first came into the program, every word out of my mouth carried a bit of ignorance. I knew nothing about getting, or staying sober, but I had an opinion about everything I heard.

I realized my foolishness when a man with several years of experience came to me and said, "I've listened to you speak and you're a lot sicker than you realize." That man is my sponsor to this day. I started listening in the meetings instead of speaking all the time. Over a period of time, I gained a little knowledge and learned to choose when to speak instead of simply vomiting out opinions.

I'm still better at prayer than I am at meditation, maybe because I like to hear my own voice, but I'm working on listening. One thing I know for sure, it's progress not perfection, and as long as I keep coming to Alcoholics Anonymous, I keep progressing.

PRINCIPLE 12

CHARITY/LOVE

Come to Me, all you who labor and are heavy laden, and I will give you rest. Take My yoke upon you and learn from Me, for I am gentle and lowly in heart, and you will find rest for your souls. (Matthew 11:28-29)

PEOPLE DON'T CARE HOW MUCH YOU KNOW UNTIL THEY KNOW HOW MUCH YOU CARE.

People don't want to know how smart you are. They don't care about how much you know. People have real problems, and they can tell whether someone cares or not. That's what matters to them. You can't be of good service to others if you don't truly care about helping them.

Sure, I can take care of this or that situation, I can give simple advice from the amount of knowledge I have, but the results my Higher Power can bring about are directly affected by my attitude and sincerity, and other people can tell. If I try to help another person, or give my advice, and I don't really care, or only care a little bit, then my help and advice will do little good because the other person can tell that I'm not genuine.

If I try to help another person or give my advice and I truly care about the person or situation, the effect will be positive because the other person can feel my genuine care. It gives them confidence in my assistance and allows my Higher Power to interact, due to our unity. People don't care about how much you know until they know how much you care, so make sure you care for those you are helping if you want real results. Besides, it only helps your life more when your attitude is right.

PRINCIPLE 12—CHARITY/LOVE

YOU CAN'T KEEP IT
UNLESS YOU GIVE IT AWAY.

Why would I give away something that I wanted to keep? It didn't make a lot of sense to me. If I've got fifty dollars, and I want to keep it, giving it away doesn't seem like a very smart way of accomplishing that. If I've got a car to drive around in, giving it away is only going to get me walking to where I need to go, but the saying isn't in reference to material things. It's about my sobriety. It's about my spirit. It's about the life I'm living.

I only get something in life if I give something from it. Time, money, love, emotion, or anything else I can think of. If I want to have it, I must share it. In other words, give it away. This is where my Higher Power really comes in. I have found that I cannot outgive God with anything, especially my sobriety.

As I share my sobriety with another alcoholic, I'm empowered in my own sobriety. There is something that fills me up inside with power, hope, and drive. When I motivate others, it motivates me to be that much more committed to my own sobriety. On those occasions when someone is helped by my counsel, I get to experience the joy it brings, both from helping another person, and from being in the will of God, as Step Eleven encourages me to be.

If you want to keep your sobriety, if you want to keep your joy, remember to give it away. Share the good things that life brings your way, and you will always be filled.

OUR TRIANGLE—
RECOVERY, UNITY, SERVICE

I love our triangle. It's unbelievably powerful! All three sides of the triangle are equal. Without any of them, I would be lost. I need to maintain my recovery to stay sane. When my mind wanders, and life gets confusing, my recovery becomes jeopardized.

I help maintain my recovery with the unity of the fellowship. I go to meetings to have regular communion with others in the program. As we recover, and unite with Alcoholics Anonymous, our spirit desires to serve, to give back. Our triangle is an amazing reminder of just how simple it works. It sits in a circle to represent that it is ongoing and never-ending.

So, our triangle, recovery, unity, and service, is what keeps me grounded and growing. My mind prospers as my recovery deepens. My body prospers as my unity deepens, and my spirit prospers as my service deepens. Recovery, unity, and service translates to mind, body, and spirit. I go to meetings to hear what the body says to the mind that sparks my spirit.

PASS IT ON

My heart, my brain, and even my very life can only contain so much. When I'm all filled up with life, nothing else can come in. There's no room left, so growth ends. If my bag is full, I can't put anything else in it. However, if I take something out of my bag, and pass it on to somebody else, suddenly, I have room in my bag to receive the next thing that comes my way.

My heart, my brain, and my life are the same. If I hold onto everything in life, I'm of no service to anyone or anything. Life becomes all about me, and I sit stagnant. If I take what I have in my heart, and pass it on, God fills my heart back up, each time, expanding it a little more. As I share what knowledge comes my way, my brain opens up and receives more bits of wisdom. When I get out of myself and share my life with others, my whole world changes.

I have found that the more of my heart, brain, and life I share with others, the more life I seem to have, and the fuller it seems to be. My entire world has become full, and my cup has run over, ever since I learned to pass it on.

IF YOU WANT TO DRINK, IT'S YOUR BUSINESS. IF YOU WANT TO STOP, IT'S OUR BUSINESS.

What a statement of hope for me to hear when I came into Alcoholics Anonymous. I knew I was home. I had never experienced any place where the people there were all about helping me. Not that I was the sole purpose for their existence, but so long as I had a sincere desire to quit drinking, they had a sincere desire to share their experience, strength, and hope with me.

They were willing to put in to my sobriety, as long as I was putting in to my sobriety. If I worked at the program, they had my back, no judgment, no pressure. If I wanted to go back out and drink, that was my business. Nobody tried to deprive me of that right. I was simply exposed to stories of the lives of other people who had lived in a manner that mirrored my life.

The difference was that they had stopped. They had found a solution to their drinking problem, and they had something I wanted. How grateful and receptive I was to find out that my desire to stop drinking was exactly the business they were in. If I wanted what they had, they had a solution for me, and a desire to teach it.

IF I SHARE MY PAIN, IT IS HALVED. IF I SHARE MY JOY, IT IS DOUBLED.

What an awesome concept to carry in life. This is so clear from my experiences that it amazes me. I never looked at this dual truth in such a simple fashion, but it has definitely been my experience in life. In fact, I think that's one of the masterful traits we find in Alcoholics Anonymous.

As the saying goes, "No man is an island," and when I try to be one, I suffer. When I hold in my pain, I carry my burdens alone, and the pain is often more than I can handle, so out comes the bottle of tolerance, and I drink till the pain is gone. The problem is my life is gone too.

When I hold in my joy, I'm selfish, and no one else reaps the benefits of my experience or has the opportunity to share in that joy. On the other hand, when I share my pain, the load seems lightened as others carry the burden with me. When I share my joy, others delight with me and even learn how to experience joy themselves.

Being a part of Alcoholics Anonymous has taught me that my life is important. Not just for me, but for the benefit of others as well. When I share my pain, it is halved, and when I share my joy, it is double. Life couldn't be better.

I CAN'T—HE CAN—I THINK I'LL LET HIM.

This is possibly the most powerful concept I've heard. It's in our promises. It says, "We will suddenly realize that God is doing for us what we could not do for ourselves." I can't. He can, so I think I'll let him. It's so basic, yet so empowering. My limits are irrelevant in the hand of God. I can only say, "I can do ALL things," if I can also add, "through Christ who strengthens me" (Ph. 4:13). He is my Higher Power!

Like it says in "How It Works," "There is One who has all power, that One is God. May you find Him now." I didn't just need a Higher Power, I already had two of those, alcohol and cocaine, and both were kicking my ass. When I saw in "How It Works," that there was One who had ALL power, I realized that was what I needed—Someone, or something, that had more power than the powers of alcohol and cocaine that were controlling me.

What a relief to know that something exists that has more power than my addictions. I immediately wanted to know all I could about my new Higher Power. I wanted to tap into that power, that freedom, that serenity, and that security. I incorporated the Third Step Prayer into my daily meditations and started letting God direct my steps. I've learned that if I put one foot in front of the other and do the next indicated thing, allowing God to always be in charge, my life seems to be far more than just tolerable; it becomes really enjoyable. So, I think I'll let Him!

PRINCIPLE 12—CHARITY/LOVE

IF NOT ME, THEN WHO?

I talk about how I live a simple life, and I actually do, but most people who know me don't see it that way. I'm often overwhelmed with responsibilities that I take on, but God seems to empower me to handle them well and work through them. I know that if God wants something done, and I don't do it, He will use a monkey if He needs to. He really doesn't need me.

My God is absolutely unlimited in His powers, and He does for me things I can't do for myself. Although I know this as a fact, I also know all He has delivered me from. I'm compelled in my innermost self to give back as much as possible. Somehow, there's a strength in me that surpasses all understanding. When I'm weak and tired and admit it to Him, I'm suddenly filled with a spirit of power and determination. As I humble myself before Him, He builds me up.

It's actually a somewhat strange phenomenon, but one I've learned not to question. When I'm asked to do something, if it's at all possible for me to take on, I just do it. Sometimes I say "Yes!" without thinking about what I've been asked, but God has never let me down. When I overwhelm myself, He either gives me strength, or He gives me rest. I hope I never stop answering the call because people need help, and it's often hard for them to ask and even harder for them to find. I allow God to use me, as flawed as I am. After all, if not me, then who?

HELP, I'M STARTING TO LIKE IT HERE!

Boy, how I can relate to that statement. When I first heard it, I literally laughed out loud. I had heard people ask how long they had to go to meetings, and the answer they got was, "Till you want to go!" I thought that was stupid. It wasn't even a real answer as far as I could tell. It seemed nothing more than a smart-ass comment. It sounded like nonsense. It was like I was being told, "Get over it! Just keep doing it, especially when you don't want to." It didn't make practical sense to me. In fact, it didn't make any sense at all.

After being in the program of Alcoholics Anonymous for a while, I found myself enjoying the meetings. They were safe. They were informative. They were stimulating, and quite often flat out entertaining. I wanted to go to the meetings. I appreciate the experience, strength, and hope that was imparted to me. I enjoyed the fellowship with like-minded people and some of the meetings I actually looked forward to with happy anticipation.

I used to enjoy going to bars and looked forward to hanging out with the drunks or doped up people. It was often colorful and entertaining, but there was always such a high price to pay. Now, I struggle being around anyone under the influence of anything mind or body altering. They're a sad bunch to watch.

I now like going to meetings and recovery functions. So, like I said, when I first heard, "Help, I'm starting to like it here," I had to laugh at its truth. If you get involved and become part of our recovery family, I believe you will like it here too!

PRINCIPLE 12—CHARITY/LOVE

IF YOU WANT TO GET CLOSE TO GOD, GET CLOSE TO HIS PEOPLE.

Now that makes sense to me. When I go to church, I like to sit in the front row. I feel like the Holy Spirit sits heaviest on the speaker, and I want to be filled with as much of His power as possible. I know God's Spirit is everywhere, including the halls of Alcoholics Anonymous, but if the power is the heaviest up front, that's where I want to be. In fact, that's where I need to be.

So, when I heard someone say, "If you want to get close to God, get close to His people," it made perfect sense to me. The question became, where do I find His people? I love church, and know God's people probably hang out there, but those people don't know me. They don't understand me, and they definitely aren't the people I can open up to about my particular disease, alcoholism. It's not that I need more than God, but when it comes to His people, I need more than an ordinary Christian.

I need a like-minded person that understands my malady and has been delivered from the same. I find them in the halls of Alcoholics Anonymous, and they have a relationship with God that is as close as anything I've ever seen. They rely on Him so much, it's infectious. They desperately need Him to navigate their lives daily. Alcoholics Anonymous draws me in on a regular basis because of my need for God's strength and guidance and the simple way those things manifest through His people in AA meetings. The closer I get to His people, the closer I get to Him.

KNOWLEDGE KEPT IS KNOWLEDGE WASTED.

What's the purpose of gaining knowledge? Is it simply to die as the smartest person in world? That doesn't seem like a very worthwhile objective. Maybe lots of knowledge is needed in order for me to navigate life easier. After all, the smarter I am, the better life choices I'll make, right? If a college education produces a better chance at success, isn't that because of the knowledge one gains in school? Put some alcohol in me and all that knowledge is pretty worthless anyway.

So, just what is the purpose of knowledge? I believe the primary reason we acquire knowledge is to impart those insights to others. My job is to be of assistance and service to others. Passing on my knowledge, which also consists of my experience, strength, and hope, is foundational to the growth of society as a whole. Not because of my wisdom, but because of the combined knowledge of all who pass it on.

If I go to my grave carrying all the knowledge I've gained over the years, having never passed that knowledge on to anyone else, that knowledge was wasted, and thus, my life was a waste. When I pass my knowledge on, others gain what I have gained, which gives purpose to my knowledge. I must share what I have, because knowledge kept is knowledge wasted.

INSULATE YOURSELF WITH THE BEST RATHER THAN ISOLATE YOURSELF FROM THE WORST.

When you isolate, you lose the benefit of others' experience. Of course, the experience of most the people I was hanging out with wasn't exactly benefiting my life. The majority of them—no, all of them—were drinking, drugging, lying, cheating, stealing, or displaying some other kind of despicable lifestyle choices. I wasn't hanging out with the best of the best; it was more like the worst of the worst.

So, when I got off by myself, it was still a bad crowd. I was just like them, that's why I hung out with them. That's where I felt comfortable instead of feeling judged. When I tried to get sober, staying away from that group of people just left me isolated with the same spirit. I was just like them. How could I stay away from the bad crowd when I was the bad crowd?

Coming into Alcoholics Anonymous put me in touch with an amazing group of people. I didn't realize how good a group it was at first, but I could tell immediately that they understood the bad crowd and seemed to know how to stay away from them. They also knew how to keep from isolating. They hung out together. They got together regularly, and together, overcame their shortcomings. They insulated themselves by staying close to one another and striving to be the best person they could be. If you want a full, successful life of joy, insulate yourself with the best, rather than isolating yourself from the worst.

TAKE THE MESS TO YOUR SPONSOR.
TAKE THE SOLUTION TO THE MEETING.

This basically spells out the need for a sponsor. Most of us show up without a clue on how to fix our lives. We are broken, hurting, and looking for a solution. We need to hear others share their experience, strength, and hope, so we can learn how to live a life of joy, instead of one of bondage. It's the members that show us the solution.

I've got this stuff in me that I need to get out, and sometimes, it just needs to come out when it needs to come out, so I don't explode! Having a sponsor gives me someone that I can let all my stuff out with. If sponsors haven't been through the same things, they have most likely observed the same in others. The experiences they have had on recovery are the things that you can use to be guided along your way.

Suddenly, you will find yourself sharing the solution in a meeting, and someone else will come to you with their stuff, asking you for help. Sponsors do not take on sponsees simply for fun. We sponsor others, because it keeps us in the middle of the herd. It ensures our sobriety, while giving back out of gratitude to the very program that saved us.

GOD LED ME TO AA, AND AA LED ME TO GOD. I NEED BOTH!

I went to seven inpatient treatment centers and I still wasn't sober. Each treatment center was followed by a relapse, which was in turn was followed by another jail sentence, which was in turn, followed by another treatment center. My life was one vicious circle. I was getting dizzy as it continued to spiral. I went to church, had hands laid on me, got anointed with oil, prayed till it hurt, and got drunk anyway. What in the world was wrong with me? Why did I always make the wrong decisions?

Through all of this, I was constantly being directed to Alcoholics Anonymous. The judge wanted me to go there. The people in treatment wanted me to go there. My family wanted me to go there. Even the church would guide me to others in recovery, who, go figure, told me to go to AA. I started to realize that every time I prayed, I would have visions and thoughts of Alcoholics Anonymous, and the people I saw within the halls. Even God was leading me to AA.

I started attending meetings with an understanding that, for me, there was no place else to go. I'd tried everything else. I purposed to thoroughly follow the path of sobriety outlined in *The Big Book* of Alcoholics Anonymous. As I followed the suggestions of my sponsor, read the literature, and worked the steps, I was led back to the One who has all power, as it tells us in "How It Works." God led me to AA, and AA led me back to God. I need both!

THERE'S A WRENCH TO FIT EVERY NUT.

I like to mess around at Evergreen Speedway because it's fairly inexpensive, yet if you use your imagination, it kind of feels like NASCAR. The track is run by NASCAR, and to drive on it, you need a NASCAR license, but it ain't the 220 mile an hour NASCAR, that's for sure. I own some cars now, and my nephew is one of my drivers. He's also a certified automotive and diesel mechanic, college degree and everything. His toolbox is taller than me. Cabinets and drawers, and pull outs, thousands of tools. Things I've never seen or heard of. I've never seen him have to borrow one. His toolbox literally has a wrench for every nut.

That's what I've found Alcoholics Anonymous to be: a giant toolbox with a wrench to fit every nut. There's a vast array of characters and personalities in our program. Most of us are nuts when we first come in. Some of us are still nuts long after, but what amazes me is all the wrenches that there are. No matter what your issue is, no matter where you've been in life, in Alcoholics Anonymous, there is someone who has been there too.

After staying in the fellowship of Alcoholics Anonymous for a while, I've seen others come in who have suffered some of the same things as me. I've even been used as a wrench to help tighten up some of their lives. I'm still a nut sometimes, but I know where to go to get straightened out. I head to my toolbox, which, for me, is a meeting of Alcoholics Anonymous, and I'm grateful that there's a wrench to fit every nut in AA.

PRINCIPLE 12—CHARITY/LOVE

GOD—GOOD ORDERLY DIRECTION: GROUP OF DRUNKS

In *The Big Book* of Alcoholics Anonymous, it states in chapter four, "We Agnostics,", that our problem is a lack of power, and that we had to find a Power greater than ourselves. Further said, it meant that we were going to talk about God. If God is a difficult concept for you, fear not, Step Three says, "God as we understand Him."

God will not be insulted if your understanding of Him is different from some church experience, or even if you have no concept of Him at all. Neither will you offend those of us who live in the program. Many of us, you will discover, once felt the same way as you.

While you find your way, God can be Good Orderly Direction, if that helps give you power. Having your focus on something else, like a plan to work through, is like being accountable to a Higher Power, because direction and purpose to your daily walk in life can give you power over wandering.

If, like me, you need something a little more hands-on, then a "Group Of Drunks" might work for a while. Leaning on the fellowship of the other members of Alcoholics Anonymous was a huge part of my path. There is something about being with them that makes me feel OK in my own skin. They understand me, which allows me to be comfortable and relaxed around them, yet they call me out on my crap too.

A Group Of Drunks is exactly what God used to get through to me. Whether it's God Himself, "Good Orderly Direction," or a "Group Of Drunks," it tells us in chapter five "How It Works" that there is One who has all power. That One is God; may you find Him now!

TRUST GOD—CLEAN HOUSE—HELP OTHERS

In that order! You can't clean your house appropriately if God, your Higher Power, hasn't directed your steps. You can't help others if your own life is a mess. So yes, trust God, clean house, and help others. In that order. I try to keep it that simple.

Every day when I wake, I need to acknowledge God. I need to realize that without Him, the best I can do is a seat in Alcoholics Anonymous. Without Him, I not only don't know the best path for my life, but I am ill-equipped to navigate where I'm at or where I'm going. Our literature tells me that there is One who has all power and that One is God, so I trust God.

Life can wreak havoc on my house. When I got here, my life was unmanageable. My house wasn't just a mess. It was a garbage dump. Every time I cleaned, it seemed to instantly get dirty again. As I put my trust in God, I grew in the program. My house wasn't as overwhelming to clean and didn't even seem to get that dirty often, or that fast. Life became bearable, then workable, and then comfortable.

I wanted to share the experience, strength, and hope I got from these growths in my life with others. My heart changed and I desired to show others the path. As I got better, I started serving in various capacities. Life gets better daily as I trust God (my Higher Power), clean house (my life), and help others (serve).

PRINCIPLE 12—CHARITY/LOVE

THEY CAN'T CUT YOU OFF
IF YOU LET THEM IN.

Not only is getting cut off in traffic irritating to me, it can also be dangerous. It can very easily cause me to react too fast and cause a wreck. Usually, though, it just gets under my skin and then I let it destroy my attitude. The rest of my commute is done with smoke coming out of my ears and cursing from my mouth. Every driver is pissing me off at that point.

What if I just let the person in instead? What if I pay attention to the drivers around me and give them the space they need, instead of having feelings like they're getting in 'my' way on 'my' road. I've actually done that once or twice, and it's kind of amazing. If I simply let them in, I seem to benefit from it. Instead of a ticked off attitude, full of anger and resentment towards the other driver, I feel a bit elated. My commute becomes relaxed, and I find patience and tolerance with all the other drivers.

My entire life is like that. I've found that when I hold to a brazen opinion and attitude, demanding that things be my way, life is contentious. Serenity doesn't surround me when I drive through life in the fast lane, denying others the right to a place on the road. Being courteous and cordial turns out to be just as good for me as it is for those I treat that way. In fact, I think I get more benefit from it than they do. I no longer get cut off in life, or traffic, because I've learned to let them in.

WHEN YOU COME INTO AA, GET A NICE SUIT.

All I thought when I first heard this was that there must be a lot of formal parties in Alcoholics Anonymous. Why else would I need a nice suit? It turns out, it was actually not for pleasurable purposes. The sad reality of our disease is the reason a nice suit will be needed.

As you stay in the fellowship awhile, you see people come in and out of the program. Unfortunately, you'll eventually see one not come back. You will find it to be respectable to wear a nice suit at that person's funeral. You see, it's a sad reality that some of us have to die so the rest of us can live. It's the reminder we get when someone can't seem to make it in sobriety, and for one reason or another, they go back out and never make it back in.

It never gets better out there; it only gets worse. If you happen to struggle yourself, if you can't give yourself fully to the program, if you can't surrender your very being to the fact you are an alcoholic, and to drink is to die, that one who doesn't come back could be you. In that case, at least you'll have something to be buried in. At least you won't leave the picking out of a suit to your loved ones. When you come into AA, get a nice suit, because you'll either be going to lots of funerals, or you'll have something to be buried in.

DON'T HIDE IT, DIVIDE IT.

Everything in my life I tried to hide became more of a problem. Holding things in would eat holes in my very soul. My life would fall through these holes and climbing out kept getting harder and harder. I would stuff things away, truly trying to make them disappear, yet they were always there. Over time, they would pop back up and start tearing me apart again. No matter what I tried to hide, it always reappeared.

Talking about them hurt and made me realize what a failure I was. So, stuff, stuff, stuff was my answer, but pain, pain, pain was the result. I just couldn't figure out how to get this stuff out of me. That was it, I had to get all of this junk out of me. Stuffing it down, holding it in, and trying to hide it was keeping it all inside. The key was to somehow let it out.

As I began to share the destructive parts of my life, as I began to let out all the things I had tried to hide, there was a release of anxiety. I have a good memory, so it's not like they disappeared altogether, but their sting was gone. I was no longer walking through life trying to be one thing and knowing inside I was something else. I was who I was, and that was okay, so long as there was some movement forward.

As I shared the bad, my life became good. I no longer hold things and let them fester and become twice as bad. I share them and let the pain hurt half as much. Don't hide it; divide it.

WHO WE ARE IS GOD'S GIFT TO US.
WHAT WE BECOME IS OUR GIFT TO GOD.

One thing I have learned in becoming sober, probably the biggest thing, is that I don't exist purely for the sake of taking up air and space. Just as we create things for certain purposes, I, too, was created for a purpose. I have a Higher Power who created me for a specific purpose. He made me who I am to fulfill that purpose.

Who I am is God's gift to me. If I follow a life in which I do what He would have me to do, there is no doubt my life will be much more easily manageable. When I chose to follow my own selfish, self-centered desires, I found out the hard way that my life became unmanageable. It is in my best interest to become what my Higher Power created me to be and to do what He created me to do.

The Big Book tells me in "How It Works," that there is One who has all power. That One is God, and I should find Him now! If He has all power, then He is the One who created me. Nobody knows better the purpose of something than the One who created it. How it pleases the Creator to see His creation becoming what it was meant to be. What I become is my gift to God. Achieving that with His guidance makes my life the best it can be.

PRINCIPLE 12—CHARITY/LOVE

AA IS ONE BEGGAR TELLING ANOTHER BEGGAR WHERE THE BREAD IS.

What a simple concept! What a simple program! I was starving for peace of mind, love, manageability, self-esteem, any amount of serenity, and had no idea where I could be fed this kind of meal. Everywhere I looked, the cupboards were empty! Then I walked into a meeting of Alcoholics Anonymous and found a literal buffet to be served from.

When I listen, I learn where to find the food I need. I get fed reading the literature. I get fed when I fellowship with others in the program. I get fed when I listen to the stories of others they share in meetings. I get fed when I play clean and sober softball, or clean and sober bowling. I get fed every time I hear the experience, strength, and hope of someone who has overcome the things that I am trying to overcome.

The hunger for peace of mind, love, manageability, self-esteem, and serenity has been satisfied. Every time a new hunger arises, I am grateful that I have a place to go, where another alcoholic can tell this alcoholic where the bread is. I came to AA hungry, and I have been fed over and over again.

FINAL THOUGHTS—
WHY WE WERE CHOSEN

God in His wisdom selected this group of men and women to be purveyors of His goodness. In selecting them, through whom to bring about this phenomenon, He went not to the proud, the mighty, the famous, or the brilliant. He went instead to the humble, to the sick, to the unfortunate. He went right to the drunkard, the so-called weakling of the world. Well might He have said the following words to us:

"Unto your weak and feeble hands, I have entrusted a power beyond estimate. To you has been given that which has been denied the most learned of your fellows. Not to scientists or statesmen, not to wives or mothers, not even to My priests or ministers have I given this gift of healing other alcoholics which I entrust to you.

"It must be used unselfishly; it carries with it grave responsibility. No day can be too long; no demands upon your time can be too urgent; no case can be too pitiful; no task too hard; no effort too great. It must be used with tolerance for I have restricted its application to no race, no creed, and no denomination. Personal criticism you must expect; lack of appreciation will be common; ridicule will be your lot; your motives will be misjudged. You must be prepared for adversity, for what men call adversity is the ladder you must use to ascend the rungs toward spiritual perfection, and remember, in the exercise of this power I shall not exact from you beyond your capabilities.

"You are not selected because of exceptional talents, and be careful always, if success attends your efforts not to ascribe to personal superiority that to which you can lay claim only by virtue of My gift. If I had wanted learned men to accomplish this mission,

PRINCIPLE 12—CHARITY/LOVE

this power would have been entrusted to the physician and scientist. If I had wanted eloquent men, there would have been many anxious for the assignment, for talk is the easiest used of all talents with which I have endowed mankind. If I had wanted scholarly men, the world is filled with better qualified men than you who would be available. You were selected because you have been the outcasts of the world and your long experience as drunkards has made or should make you humbly alert to the cries of distress that come from the lonely hearts of alcoholics everywhere."[2]

ENDNOTES

1. https://quotefancy.com/quote/878496/Og-Mandino-I-will-not-allow-yesterday-s-success-to-lull-me-into-today-s-complacency-for

2. "Why We Were Chosen." Speech by Judge John T., 4th Anniversary of the Chicago Group, Alcoholics Anonymous, 1943.